LITURGICAL LITERACY:

From ANAMNESIS to WORSHIP

DENNIS C. SMOLARSKI, S.J.

PAULIST PRESS
NEW YORK / MAHWAH

IMPRIMI POTEST
April 4, 1989
Very Rev. Paul F. Belcher, S.J., Provincial
California Province, Society of Jesus

Copyright ©1990 by
Jesuit Community at Santa Clara University

All rights reserved. No part of this book may be reproduced or transmitted in any form or by any means, electronic or mechanical, including photocopying, recording, or by any information storage and retrieval system without permission in writing from the Publisher.

Library of Congress Cataloging-in-Publication Data

Smolarski, Dennis Chester, 1947–
    Liturgical literacy : from anamnesis to worship / by Dennis C. Smolarski.
       p. cm.
    Includes bibliographical references.
    ISBN 0-8091-3137-4
    1. Catholic Church—Liturgy—Dictionaries. 2. Liturgics—Dictionaries. I. Title.
BV173.S66   1990
264'.02'003—dc20   89-48552
                                                                                      CIP

Published by Paulist Press
997 Macarthur Boulevard
Mahwah, New Jersey 07430

Printed and bound in the
United States of America

CONTENTS

Preface	1
Chapter 1 – Liturgical Literacy	3
Chapter 2 – From Anamnesis to Worship	10
Chapter 3 – From Thanksgiving back to Epiclesis	15
Chapter 4 – From Past to Future	18
Chapter 5 – Overview	30
Chapter 6 – Foundations: List 1	35
Chapter 7 – Contemporary Fluency: List 2	37
Chapter 8 – Historical and Technical Proficiency: List 3	43
Chapter 9 – The Dictionary	48
Bibliography	208

*In memory of
all those who laid the foundation
for liturgical literacy,
especially*
Lambert Beauduin, O.S.B.
and
Josef A. Jungmann, S.J.

Αἰωία ὑμῶν ἡ μνήμη

Eternal be your memory!

—taken from the Byzantine funeral liturgy

PREFACE

The difficulty of communicating intelligently is a phenomenon that has only recently awakened the interest of experts in various fields. One part of the difficulty in this communication process involves the categories that people use to express their thoughts. Another part of the difficulty involves the limited catalogues of concepts and words that people possess as part of their backgrounds, concepts and words that they are able to use in communicating their thoughts. It is the well-turned phrase, scriptural allusion, or quotation from Shakespeare, that makes the reading of great authors more satisfying than the reading of the morning newspaper.

This book attempts to aid intelligent communication about public worship by focusing on *liturgical literacy*, which, I suggest, is the ability to read about and intelligently discuss the community's public adoration of its God. Such discussion should be done with a respect for and knowledge of history, scripture, tradition, and human nature. My hope is that our understanding of the nature of contemporary worship may be improved if we make use of the various forms of human communication available to us, especially oral and visual forms, and if we expand our vocabulary and our understanding of the words and objects we use in worship. We need to speak and read about worship, both past and present, in order to improve our future relationship with God. By our coming to a deeper understanding of what we do when we gather for worship, the vision that was proclaimed by the bishops of the Second Vatican Council may become ever more and more a reality in our world.

However, *liturgical literacy* is only a small part of a larger question. It is hard to become literate in a special area if one is not literate in general. In other words, as Aidan Kavanagh, O.S.B. wrote me, "one who is *culturally* illiterate is going to find being *liturgically* literate almost impossible."

My special thanks go to those who have inspired me by their own writings on liturgy, and those who have helped in developing the various literacy lists that are contained in this work. In particular, I would like to thank Michael Moynahan, S.J. and his class in Christian Liturgy at Santa Clara University (Fall Quarter, 1988) for their work in suggesting terms that should form a core set on which to build literacy. In addition, I would like to acknowledge Msgr. Joseph Champlin, Robert Hamma, J. Frank Henderson, Aidan Kavanagh, O.S.B., Michael Kwatera, O.S.B., Georgia Mandakas, Thomas J. Talley, and Eugene A. Walsh, S.S. for their help in expanding and fine-tuning the various lists of words. I would also like to acknowledge Rita Claire Dorner, O.P., Paul Halmos, Arthur Liebscher, S.J., and Edward V. Warren, S.J. for the insightful comments and editorial suggestions given after reading earlier drafts of the text.

CHAPTER 1
LITURGICAL LITERACY

When Eric D. Hirsch, Jr. published his controversial book *Cultural Literacy* in 1987, he did a great service by suggesting that literacy goes beyond merely being able to read and write. Indeed, we cannot take even those basic skills for granted, as recent television advertisements about illiteracy too vividly remind us. Hirsch proposed that contemporary people should be exposed to a body of handy knowledge in order to appreciate the achievements of the past and make similar progress for the future. Controversy entered in specifying the items included in such a "literacy" list and, thus, in determining what the content of that body of knowledge should be. Even in the one year between the publication of the hardbound version of Hirsch's book (1987) and the appearance of a paperback version (1988), there were a significant number of additions to the "literacy" list in his book—and a few omissions as well. What may also be controversial is the meaning attached to words listed—the same word may have different fundamental meanings to different individuals. Nevertheless, Hirsch's thesis remains intact. We need a certain basic content of knowledge held in common for us to understand each other and to appreciate allusions to the great cultural events of the past and the present. One wonders how many "typical" high school students today would be able to find *half* of the allusions contained in the famous "I have a dream" speech of Dr. Martin Luther King—would phrases from Scripture stand out as readily today as they did in the 1960's when the speech was written and given? There is so much interest in this topic in some academic circles that some schools are developing curricula based on the *Cultural Literacy* list, and making use of Hirsch's second volume, *The Dictionary of Cultural Literacy*, as a starting point for further studies.

"Literacy" affects many other areas of human existence as well. Many schools are suggesting that students need a basic course in "computer literacy" to be able to qualify for any sort of job today, from sales clerk to secretary to medical technician. Mathematics teachers (like myself) bemoan the backgrounds of our students when we attempt to teach a first course in Calculus—many seem to be "illiterate" about the basic rules of arithmetic and the basic concepts of algebra. For many people today, it seems that "sine" and "cosine" have nothing to do with right triangles, but are only buttons on a calculator. I nearly collapse and weep when I remember the hours I spent thumbing through tables of logarithms to do a messy numerical algebra problem in the early 1960's, yet contemporary high school graduates are never taught these "hallowed" logarithmic procedures, since modern pocket calculators have made the use of logarithms almost unnecessary.

The world has changed much since the end of World War II, and much of that process of change has accelerated since the 1960's, the time of the Second Vatican Council and the Vietnam war. We must be familiar with the discoveries of the 1980's, yet not ignore the wonders of the 1880's. Unfortunately, unless we have a common language about our past, we may not be able to build a future. Some statistics from Hirsch's book about one measure of literacy, the scores on the S.A.T. (Scholastic Aptitude Test), should be particularly disturbing. Over the 8 year period, from 1976 to 1984, the percentage of high scores (scores over 600 and scores over 650) dropped to nearly *half*.[1] Not all of this decline could be attributed to more teenagers (with a greater variation in backgrounds) taking the exam either, as statistics from the Second International Mathematics Study have shown.[2]

It is my conviction that *awareness* is the first stage in any sort of solution for problems, whether those problems are cultural or of another kind. Unless we are *aware* of deficiencies, we cannot do much to overcome them. Hirsch has made us aware of a fundamental problem in our educational systems—how to *overcome* the problem is a different question.

In reflecting on Hirsch's basic thesis, it occurred to me that a similar deficiency may be affecting liturgical renewal in the Christian Churches today. Much has been written about the revitalization of the liturgy in the last 25 years, but some very fine suggestions have been ignored, perhaps due to misunderstandings or "illiteracy" about what was actually being said. To renew our Church, and have it renew our world, we must know what we are talking about, and know the various allusions to Scripture, liturgical traditions, and the customs of various peoples. It does no good to write about music in the liturgy, when one pastor's idea of "good" music is a Palestrina Mass sung by a professionally-trained choir, and another's is a congregation singing "Sons of God, hear his holy word, . . . eat his body, drink his blood."

For many Catholics of an older generation, clerics and laity alike, "liturgy" meant "rubrics." A good liturgy was one in which not too many mortal sins were committed because of violations of the *Rítus Servandus in celebratione Missæ*, the document at the front of every Tridentine Missal that prescribed the details of the rite of Mass. For those of the middle generation, many "babies" were thrown out with the "bathwater" in the reaction against the rigid rubricism that was common prior to the late 1960's. Relevance and experimentation was "in"; tradition (even good traditions) was out. The rigidity of a single official eucharistic prayer of the 1570 Missal was augmented by the relative freedom of four official eucharistic prayers in the Missal of 1970, and of, perhaps, 400 unofficial additional prayers found in various privately published ("underground") collections. Catholics of the youngest generation have the benefit of numerous recent scholarly studies about the history of liturgy, the reasons for the changes, the spirit of the revised liturgy, and the interaction between liturgy and life, but the *example* of their elders may influence them more than the *printed words* of books or articles they read. However, each of these three generations has a religious and liturgical vocabulary of its own, and very little in common with the other two groups. Technical words that may have been commonplace for members of one age group may never have been heard by members of another. Among these technical words are, for example, *bugia* and *epiclesis* (both of which appear in the dictionary that follows). How many younger members of a parish liturgy committee have ever heard of a *bugia*, much less seen one? How many older priests have read about the relation between *anamnesis* and *epiclesis* (or care to)?

In addition, our world and our Church have changed much in the last twenty-five years, to the point where the clergy are not the only ones in many parishes who are trained in liturgical matters or who make major decisions about the way the local community worships. In some parts of North America, Catholic communities have no residential priest, and the weekly worship is conducted by deacons or lay leaders of prayer. Whoever leads or helps plan the prayer of the local community must be at least minimally conversant in the vocabulary found in the ritual books, and ideally, has enough background to do further reading in the area of liturgy and worship. However, the background of people in the pew is as varied as the background of the clerics behind the altar. A young mother who was recently hired as the Director of Religious Education for a parish may have completed a seminary program and earned a Master's degree in Religious Studies. Meanwhile, the head of the parish Liturgy Committee may have grown up with the Latin Mass and only attended a one-day seminar on planning liturgies in the contemporary Church. How do people with various backgrounds and various prejudices talk to one another about a topic as important as how the Church worships its God? Are the chasms that seem to separate us permanent barriers to any dialogue and learning?

My concern is to try to bridge the apparent gap, in a way similar to what E. D. Hirsch has done. I would like to see the existence of a basic "liturgical literacy" that forms the foundation of knowledge for all those intimately involved in Christian worship. This term, "liturgical literacy," has been used by others. In 1985, Robert J. McClory wrote an article in the *National Catholic Reporter* entitled "Scholars say liturgy still a mystery." He concluded by stating:

> Near the end of their peace pastoral, the U.S. bishops in 1982 urged the faithful to pray and fast for nuclear disarmament because of the danger the arms race poses. If they were truly formed in the liturgy, several liturgists have argued, they would have *begun* the pastoral with the argument, "Because we are a people who pray and fast, we cannot condone the nuclear arms race," and proceeded from there. In such poignant subtleties lies the genius and elusiveness of *liturgical literacy*.[3]

David Holeton, Anglican Professor of Liturgics at Trinity College of Toronto, recently wrote:

> The first need . . . in the shared liturgical ministry of bishops is the need to find candidates for advanced liturgical studies so that the general level of *liturgical literacy* might be increased in both our colleges and parishes.[4]

My suggested approach to achieve a "liturgical literacy" is similar to the approach used by Hirsch. What I have compiled is a series of lists, containing over 650 terms old and new, popular and scholarly. These are terms that I and others have found helpful in the study of liturgy, and these terms seem to be good and needed for people of the 1980's and 1990's to know as we prepare for the liturgy, Church, and society of the next millennium. In addition to the basic lists, there is a chapter of definitions or brief explanations of these terms.

All good teachers know that they must start with solid basics. Jesus as a good teacher tried that, and even suggested an image from the construction industry: building a house on rock rather than on sand. Unfortunately, the students of Jesus could not understand many of his fundamental teachings, and I am not sure how much the world has advanced.

As with other lists, choices for entries had to be made, and I am agreeable to suggestions for additions, deletions, and corrections. I have attempted to provide categories in which thought may develop and growth in knowledge can take place. The words we use create the atmosphere or ambience in which we come to know ourselves, our world, and our God more intimately. My fundamental hope is that the basis of themes and concepts that these lists provide will help all Christians, both young and old, both clergy and laity, grasp the concerns that the Church has always cherished whenever we gather to worship our loving God, the one whom Jesus called "Abba."

NOTES

1. Hirsch, *Cultural Literacy*, Chapter 1, Note 6.
2. *The Underachieving Curriculum: Assessing U.S. School Mathematics from an International Perspective*, A National Report on the Second International Mathematics Study of the International Association for the Evaluation of Education Achievement, Champaign, IL: Stripes Publishing Co., 1987, pp. 59–61.
3. Final italics mine. *National Catholic Reporter*, December 27, 1985, pp. 1, 17.
4. Italics mine. "The Bishop Leading His Diocese," Chapter 3 of *The Bishop in Liturgy: An Anglican symposium on the role and task of the bishop in the field of liturgy*, edited by (Bishop) Colin Buchanan (Bramcote: Grove Books Ltd., 1988), p. 28.

CHAPTER 2
FROM ANAMNESIS TO WORSHIP

The dictionary that follows in Chapter 9 combines all the terms in the three separate lists of Chapters 6, 7 and 8. In this master dictionary list, there are two key words (at least in my mind). One of these key words is *anamnesis* and it occurs near the beginning of the dictionary, and the other is *worship* which occurs near the end. Thus, the "dictionary of liturgical literacy" basically goes from *anamnesis* to *worship*, and so does the flow of our liturgies and our life. This chapter offers a few thoughts about that flow.

The Greek word *Anamnesis,* ’Ανάμνησις, is a noun derived from the verb "remember." In the Christian liturgical context, it refers to "active" remembrance, as described in Scripture in Exodus 13:8 ("And you shall tell your son on that day: 'It is because of what the Lord did for *me* when *I* left Egypt' "), Deuteronomy 6:23 ("He brought *us* out of there in order to lead *us* to, and give *us*, this land which He had promised to our forefathers"), and Romans 6:3–4 ("When we were baptized in Christ Jesus, we were baptized in his death. In other words, when we were baptized *we* went into the tomb with him and joined him in death, so that as Christ was raised from the dead by the Father's glory, we too might live a new life").[1] In these cases, the present is brought into intimate contact with the past, and the past with the present. The worshiper not only "remembers" the past (as

Americans might remember the Boston Tea Party), but also comes into contact with the saving event in a personal way that makes the effects of the historical event present and effective for the believer. This Greek word tries to capture what the Hebrew word *zikkaron* means, as captured in the Hebrew Scripture mentioned above.

Christian worship is fundamentally an *anamnesis*. It is an "active" remembrance of the paschal mystery—our salvation through Christ's death and resurrection. The mystery was first summarized in the celebration of a special meal, the Last Supper. In Luke's account of the Last Supper (22:19), and in Paul's description of the Last Supper tradition in his first letter to the Corinthians (11:24), we find the Greek word *anamnesis* used in the Lord's final command: "Do this in *anamnesis* of me." It is the glorious event of life-through-death that gives meaning to all of Christian worship. In the liturgy of the hours, Psalm 136 is given a subtitle from the writings of Cassiodorus, "We praise God by *recalling* his marvelous deeds."[2] This sentence summarizes the ultimate content of Christian worship.

In Matthew's Gospel, Jesus rebukes the disciples for *not* remembering (16:9, "Do you not yet understand, and do you *not remember* the five loaves for the five thousand, and how many baskets you took up?"). Especially in Matthew, the gospel narrative is written so that the hearer's present situation is seen in the history of the Lord's own life. Thus, the contemporary believer receives strength from *remembering* God's power present and active throughout all of human history.

Whether or not we are conscious of it, Christ's death and resurrection are present at every sacrament, at every celebration of the liturgy of the hours, at every blessing. Our worship of God is based on our *anamnesis* of Christ's *Pascha*, and it is the power of that dying and rising that flows into the gathered assembly. The paschal mystery is the new covenant, the fulfillment of the first Passover and exodus. It gives life and meaning to every joy that caps experiences of growth and pain.

But Christ's life was more than the sacred three days of Holy Thursday night through Easter Sunday morning. Christ's life was more than one special meal celebrated the night before he died. Thus, our remembrance of Christ must include more than merely remembering one special meal or even three special days. Christ's life was a series of events, including proclaiming divine graciousness, exhorting to a renewed relationship with God, sharing meals with tax-collectors, healing the sick, and forgiving sinners. And Christ's life (and death) was only one way (albeit a profoundly significant and definitive way) that God's love has been shown to the human race throughout recorded history. The divine love was first manifest at creation which overflowed with goodness. It was manifest at the exodus, and at the return from Babylon. It was manifest at the peace of Constantine and at the discovery of the New World. It was manifest at the end of World War I and at the end of World War II. It is shown in the love of someone like Francis of Assisi, and Mother Teresa of Calcutta. All of this is the context that colors the Christian worship experience.

To celebrate, we must remember something worth celebrating. Americans look back to 1776 each year at July 4 and the signing of the Declaration of Independence. Every individual looks back to one special day out of 365 and counts that as a birthday. Remembering is part and parcel of celebrating, and celebrating is what worship is about. We remember who we are in relation to our God, and we remember who God is in relation to us. But our remembering is not merely lifeless and passive. It is not merely like the concrete and marble monuments that honor the heroes of ages past.

From Anamnesis to Worship

Our remembering is active, or "anamnetic." We rarely pray merely to "God." We almost always pray to a God "who is merciful and compassionate," a God "who is shepherd and guide," a God "who calls us before we were born," a God "who gave us a son, the only-begotten one, born before the ages." The God we pray to made "light from darkness," made us in the divine "image and likeness," and is "love" itself.

But besides remembering God, we also remember our history. We remember our humanness, brokenness, and failures. We remember our cultural and Christian heritage. We remember childhood memories of statues and crucifixes, of dark churches and scary confessionals. We remember what made us feel closer to God and what kept us away from that Divine Lover. We remember our confusion at the discrepancies between Christ and Christians. We remember our anger at being told about norms of behavior and not seeing very many acting in accordance with those norms.

Our memory and remembering, our *anamnesis,* is what makes our worship possible and fruitful. Remembering forms the ambience and context for God to be praised and for us to celebrate. By recalling our personal history, our contemporary minds are able to form the memory that gives us solace, challenges our complacency, makes us smile, and brings forth tears. By recalling its communal history, the local Christian community is able to speak a common language when it gathers on the *Lord's Day* to celebrate and remember what it is. For whenever Christians gather for worship, ultimately they remember what Jesus did for our world, and render praise and thanks to the God of all creation who through Jesus creates and sustains each of us.

From anamnesis to worship—that is the flow of Christian life. We remember and we celebrate. We remember what God has done, and we worship the God who acts.

From God and to God—this is the spiral that draws every Christian closer and closer to God and to other Christians assembled together for worship. That is why our common religious "cultural" history is so important to know and share—our future union with God and with all our sisters and brothers in Christ depends on it.

NOTES

1. Cf. Dennis C. Smolarski, S.J., *Eucharistia: A Study of the Eucharistic Prayer*. New York: Paulist Press, 1982, pp. 67–70.

2. Evening Prayer from Monday of Week IV.

CHAPTER 3
FROM THANKSGIVING
BACK TO EPICLESIS

The rhythm of our world includes repetition and regularity, and our lives imitate that rhythm. Sunrise leads to sunset, which leads back to sunrise. In our relationship with God, we move from divine activity to human response, and from human activity back to God. In our public communal activity as Christians, we go from *anamnesis* to worship, but also back from worship to God. In the previous chapter, we moved from *anamnesis*, near the beginning of the alphabetical list of terms, to *worship*, near the end. In this chapter, we move from *thanksgiving*, a word near the end, back to *epiclesis*, a word near the beginning.

Christian prayer reaches a high point in the celebration of the mass or *eucharist*, derived from the Greek word for *thanksgiving*. But thanksgiving flows into invocation of God and a request that God accept the prayer being offered by the worshipping community. This eucharistic invocation has traditionally been given the title of *epiclesis*, a Greek word meaning "calling upon." In moving from *anamnesis* into a worship of praise and thanksgiving and then back to invocation, the Christian community follows a pattern found in the Hebrew Scriptures. We see the same pattern in the prayers for the dedication of the Jerusalem temple by Solomon, found in 1 Kings 8 and in 2 Chronicles 6. This is the pattern of prayer used in the *birkat ha-mazon*, the Jewish grace after meals, which is the ancestor of our Christian eucharistic prayer. And invocation and petition of God in prayer reaches a certain perfection in the priestly prayer of Jesus in John's Gospel, chapter 17.[1]

In the Christian Scriptures, prayer to God is related to the presence of the Holy Spirit, who makes intercession for us in groanings that we cannot understand (Rom 8:26). It is the Spirit that enables us to call upon God as "Abba" (Gal 4:6). It is the presence of God that enables us even to remember God's action in our lives. In reading the *Confessions* of St. Augustine, one can realize that God is very much present within human memory, and to remember is to prayerfully invoke the Holy One in the power of the Spirit. *Anamnesis* is worship, which in turn is *epiclesis*. As Nathan Mitchell, O.S.B. wrote:

> The purpose of the epicletic invocation in the sacraments is *not* to supply something lacking in memorial, but to reveal in the external life of the Christian people what is already enfleshed in their collective memory. *Anamnesis* and *epiclesis* in the sacraments are not separable items; they are the outside and the inside of a single reality—the reality of God's Word become flesh, the reality of Christ's broken body becoming a body corporate. Thus, for example, to "do the memorial of Christ's passover" in the Christian eucharist is, at the same time, to invoke the Spirit who exhibits *both* gifts *and* people as the tangible flesh of what that paschal memorial means.[2]

It is the Spirit who came upon Mary at the Annunciation, and upon Jesus at his Baptism. It is the Spirit who gathers the Christian assembly together to give praise and thanks to God through Jesus. In our worship, we invoke God that we may always realize the divine presence and the power of the Spirit in our lives, whether that power be the agent which transforms earthly bread and wine into divine nourishment, or that power be the agent which gathers numerous individuals and unites them into the one body of Christ. It is the irony of God's interaction with the human race, that we cannot even begin to pray without the Spirit, but in our prayer, we are led back to petitioning for the Spirit as the first of many requests.

The rhythm of our prayer moves from *anamnesis* to *worship* through *thanksgiving* to *epiclesis* back to *anamnesis*. It is a cycle begun with God and leading back to God, and we are so much the happier for being caught up in its spiral.

NOTES

1. Cf. Dennis C. Smolarski, S.J., *Eucharistia: A Study of the Eucharistic Prayer*. New York: Paulist Press, 1982, pp. 78–83.

2. Nathan Mitchell, O.S.B., "Christian Initiation: Decline and Dismemberment," *Worship* (v. 48 [1974], n. 8), pp. 478–9.

CHAPTER 4
FROM PAST TO FUTURE

We need to remember—very few people will debate that. But what can be debated is the influence that remembering our history should have in determining our actions in the present as we move toward planning the future. We take history courses in school not to live in the past, but to learn from it. We learn about our roots, not to stay stuck in the mud, but to bear new fruit in the freedom of the air surrounding us.

Our past shapes our future, not like a metal form for a concrete pillar but like a recipe for a fine pastry. When we remember the recipe correctly and purify our ingredients, the result is a source of wonder and delight. When the text of the recipe becomes worn or blurred or when pieces of it become lost, the result is often far from what is desired. Something similar happens with our past. The recipes that shape our liturgical gatherings often become blurred with the passage of time and need to be cleaned up and infused with the ingredients of the era in which we live. All the while we must not neglect the origins from which these gatherings sprang and the purpose that they serve.

Too often, when people remember the past, they get stuck in a nostalgia that inhibits growth. They remember the past through the haze of many years—the view of reality is clouded by uncertain facts and wishful thinking. This phenomenon is sometimes reflected in the words we use. Meanings of words develop and change, yet some people have not adjusted to the reality of the present and stay caught in an unreal past. Some people long for the liturgy of the 1940's with Latin Masses and Gregorian chant. Others long for the liturgy of the 140's in the houses of the faithful, with ordinary clothes, ordinary bread, ordinary wine. However, neither the recent nor the far distant past by themselves helps us really understand the liturgy of today. By themselves they cannot help us shape the liturgy of tomorrow, either. We need to reflect on and develop our understanding of who we are as God's holy people and how we are to worship God, through Christ our Redeemer, empowered by the Spirit of Love. And with this renewed understanding, we can then incorporate past practices into our present world, as we look toward the next century. We need to know what a word meant to early Christians, and what that same word should mean to Christians of the coming millennium. All this involves liturgical literacy.

As one of the founders of the liturgical movement, Dom Bernard Botte, O.S.B., wrote in his autobiography, "to understand a movement, you have to know its starting point."[1] Liturgical literacy involves knowing about our origins and our past history, and then realizing the growth and development that has taken place over the years. Thus, liturgical literacy necessarily involves knowing some of the fundamentals of liturgical history. One cannot truly appreciate the progress of liturgical renewal since the Second Vatican Council unless one realizes that at the beginning of the twentieth century, it was commonly thought that the purpose of the Mass was to refill the tabernacle. Until the 1960's, devotion to the eucharist outside of Mass was considered more important by most Catholics than devotion within Mass. It is recounted that at the beginning of the twentieth century someone who had a doctorate in theology considered that it was better to receive communion immediately before Mass from the tabernacle, and then to use the Mass as a period of thanksgiving, rather than to receive communion during the Mass itself![2]

We are attaining a new era of liturgical literacy, and much of it is due to the great historical studies by people like Josef Jungmann, S.J. and Dom Gregory Dix. Because of these studies, the Church, through its pastors gathered at the Second Vatican Council, realized that some of our thoughts and attitudes about liturgical matters needed changing, and thus numerous changes in practices were actually introduced into the 1969 Order of Mass approved by Paul VI. In many cases, the reasons for these changes were *not* explained well enough, and because of this, the hoped-for renewal has been slower than some people thought it might or should be.

Thomas S. Kuhn, author of *The Structure of Scientific Revolutions*, uses the title "paradigm" to describe a *system* or *model* used by scientists to describe some aspect of our world.[3] He then speaks about a "paradigm-shift," which is a change in the understanding of the underlying *pattern* or *schema* we use to evaluate and interact with something. A standard scientific example of such a shift is the change from Ptolemy's view of the universe (with the earth at the center of our solar system) to that of Copernicus and Galileo (with the sun at the center). A paradigm can affect human actions, for if you view the world as flat, you may hesitate to sail too far away from the shore. It can affect relationships and attitudes as well.

Although Kuhn uses paradigm in speaking about science, it can be used in other contexts as well. When learning languages with numerous declensions and conjugations, students memorize the declension of certain words as paradigms in order to learn how to modify the endings for other words. We also know what can happen when our paradigms are not correct. Asking for a "lift" in the United States usually means seeking a ride, while in Great Britain it is a request for the nearest elevator. This difference in the meaning of words can be viewed as a version of a paradigm-shift, especially if the change in meaning is due to a broader way in which we view the world in which we find ourselves.

I suggest that, in one sense, what took place in the liturgical revolution from the 1950's to the 1970's was a similar paradigm-shift, and any major paradigm shift involves difficulties. It is not easy to shift from viewing the world as *flat* to viewing it as a *sphere*. It is not easy to shift from seeing the earth as the center of the universe to seeing the sun as the center of our tiny solar system. We continue to say "the sun rises and sets" even though we know the earth is moving and not the sun. Unfortunately, with the liturgy, we often still act as if the earth were the center of the universe in the way we carry out certain ritual actions. Paradigm shifts have occurred in the Church before. For example, the Council of Florence in 1450 decreed that the matter and form of ordination consisted in the handing of instruments with the accompanying formula. It seems that Thomas Aquinas assumed that position as well. Today, that understanding embarrasses us. We now hold that ordination is conferred by the imposition of hands and by prayer, and we also hold that the matter of any sacrament is unchangeable throughout the ages.

What are the various paradigms that affect our understanding of the word *word*? To some, a word is viewed primarily as a concept, which is only secondarily verbalized. This seems to be the way that it is used in the prologue of St. John's Gospel. To others it is a series of audible vibrations. To others it is a series of visible symbols, such as what is printed on a piece of paper. And to many people nowadays, *word* is primarily an electronic unit used by computers for remembering information. What will the beginning of St. John's Gospel mean in a few years to people whose primary paradigm of *word* is electronic?

On a non-religious level, many of us have been forced to make shifts regarding the meaning of words even within the last decade. *Boot* used to be a noun referring to footwear. More and more frequently, *boot* is a verb that designates the initialization process performed when computers are first turned on. Nowadays, some people are more concerned about the *footprint* that a computer makes on a desk than about *footprints* of mud that children track across the living room carpet. We all deal with shifts in meaning, and most of us have made these various transitions without too many scars in our psyche.

The work of liturgical historians has been accepted and enfleshed in our revised liturgical books. However, in many ways, many who use these books unconsciously have *not* made the shift to a new paradigm. We may have new words, but some of us retain old mentalities, and much of it is not our fault. In most instances, the new vision has never been systematically described or perhaps never been properly understood. This is another aspect of contemporary liturgical literacy. Not only should people possess a common vocabulary, but the underlying meaning of the words they use should be the same as well.

When I celebrate the eucharist in a Byzantine Rite Church, I consciously have to make paradigms shifts. I have often wondered if an even greater paradigm shift took place between the old Roman Missal and the present Roman Missal, than takes place between the Roman Rite and the Byzantine Rite. Many people would agree that it would be problematic trying to celebrate a Roman Rite Mass correctly in a Byzantine church, primarily because the architecture is not conducive to the Roman Rite. I wonder if many of our older

Roman Rite churches are also still ill-suited to celebrating the revised Roman Rite Mass, because those in charge of certain churches are using the vocabulary of the *new* liturgy but with *old* meanings and thus exhibit a certain "liturgical *il*literacy."

Many of the ritual changes introduced in the 1960's and 1970's are based on historical studies of liturgy and are well-founded, at least from the academic perspective. Yet, because many of us are still accustomed to older explanations and patterns, the revised ritual asks us to do things contrary to what may still be part of our personal piety, or to what was written in older liturgical manuals. As a result, certain parts of our liturgies may appear to lack a certain flow or spirit, because of differing paradigms competing in our subconscious as we try to move through the rite.

As a concrete example of a liturgical paradigm shift let us analyze the second half of the Mass—what we used to call the Mass of the Faithful. My eighth grade *Baltimore Catechism* (with copyright date 1941) has the question: "Which are the principal parts of the Mass of the Faithful?" The answer includes the *offertory* (which included the preface and *Sanctus*); the *consecration* (which included the *Agnus Dei*); and the *communion* (which included the last blessing and last gospel).[4]

This summarized the old interpretation of the liturgy of the eucharist, formerly called the "Mass of the Faithful." It consisted of three parts: the offertory, the consecration, and the communion. Today, we realize that that division is inaccurate. Moreover, if we unconsciously build our actions on that paradigm, we may be actually doing damage to the spirit of the revised liturgy.

The second half of the Mass is now seen as having two main sections: the liturgy of the eucharist and the concluding rite. And through the efforts of Dom Gregory Dix and others, we realize that the liturgy of the eucharist is further subdivided into *four* "movements" (to borrow a term from the world of music). And these "movements" are not arbitrary divisions; they are based on a careful reading of the gospels and Paul's first letter to the Corinthians. In the Last Supper account found in the synoptics (e.g., Mt 26:26) and in Paul (1 Cor 11:23–24), in the accounts of the multiplication of the loaves in Matthew (e.g. Mt 14:19), and in the Emmaus account in Luke (24:30), we find four verbs appearing repeatedly with such prominence and regularity that we suspect the repetition is due to liturgical influence. Over and over again we read that Jesus *took* bread, *blessed* God for that gift, *broke* the bread, and *shared* or *gave* it to others.

This new interpretation has been given official recognition in the *General Instruction of the Roman Missal*, paragraph 48, where those four verbs form the basis of the present vision of the liturgy of the eucharist. The preparation of the gifts ritualizes Christ's *taking*, the eucharistic prayer repeats this *blessing* (which is not split as in the *Baltimore Catechism*), the *Agnus Dei* accompanies the *breaking of the bread*, and the *sharing* takes place through communion. For us to base our eucharistic practice on a different format, we would have to ignore the best of recent biblical and liturgical scholarship and also ignore what we find written in the revised liturgical books themselves.

Of the four biblical verbs, only one is related to words: "bless." The other three are actions: "take, break, share." If we do have words at those action moments, the words must be secondary to the ritual *action*. In addition, of these four verbs, two are principal (*blessing* and *sharing*) and two are preparatory (*taking* must precede *blessing*, and *breaking* must precede *sharing*).

So much for background—what are the practical consequences? Let us look at two examples.

First let us examine the preparation of the gifts of bread and wine at the altar. In the revised Missal, there is a drastically different meaning associated with the ritual surrounding putting the bread and wine on the altar. In the 1570 Missal, this rite was an "offering." The priest had to hold the paten and chalice at eye level and say prayers that mentioned "offering." That was the common interpretation of what was supposed to occur at this point of Mass, but it seems to have had no theological, biblical or historical justification. In a sense, like Ptolemy, this interpretation mistook the center of its universe.

In the present Missal, the revised rite is entitled "Preparation of the Gifts." The paten and chalice are supposed to be held only a few inches above the altar, and the revised translations of the Hebrew-style prayers in other languages do not even mention "offer" as the present English texts do. In fact, in the *General Instruction of the Roman Missal*, "offering" is only used to refer to a section of the eucharistic prayer after the consecration.

We have essentially had a paradigm shift, at least in theory. However, has this shift in theory truly affected our liturgical practice, or do the *Baltimore Catechism* and our personal piety influence our actions more than the rubrics of the revised Missal?

The explanation given above about the structure of the liturgy of the eucharist in the revised Missal attempted to show that the rite of preparing the gifts is not as important a section of the Mass as the eucharistic prayer. It also is *not* primarily a verbal section. Nor does it have to do with offering. It has a lot to do with "taking" the bread and wine (the "matter" of the eucharist). The preparation of the gifts is a simple action by which we recall Christ's *taking* of bread, wine, and fish during his life. What is important is an action —the action of the presider receiving the bread and wine and reverently placing them on the altar. These gifts are received from Christ's followers, and they are prepared for the eucharistic prayer to come by making physical contact with the altar, the abiding symbol of Christ in the church. That physical contact between the plate with the bread and the cup with the wine should take place only once. An elongated ritual of receiving the gifts from the people, placing them on the altar once, lifting them high, then putting them on the altar a second time, does not make much sense in terms of contemporary paradigm given in the revised Missal.

The new paradigm, as enfleshed in the revised vision of the preparation of the gifts, has several implications:

—The preparation rite is primarily *action*—words should be secondary, ideally should not be heard by the assembly, and can even be misleading (although the prayers are beautiful).

—The preparation rite is *not* an offering—the offering takes place during the eucharistic prayer. Hence, gestures of *offering* during which the gifts are raised high are inappropriate.

—The preparation rite is secondary to the eucharistic prayer. It is not an equal. Words and gestures of "offering" during this time are secondary to the important action of *taking* the *gifts* and *placing* them on the corporal.

—The prayers of the preparation rite are prayers of "placement" (i.e., prayers to accompany *placing* the gifts on the altar) and not prayers of "offering."

In our revised books, we have been given a new paradigm of what the second half of the Mass is about. It may be difficult for some to make the adjustment, but keeping the old paradigm alive may be no more fruitful than being a member of the Flat Earth Society.

Now, some might object that the Fathers of the Church spoke about the faithful bringing gifts for the "offering." I would counter by suggesting that if "offering" is understood as referring to the eucharistic prayer with its statement of "offering" (normally occurring after the "consecration"), an entirely different evaluation of what the Fathers are saying is possible. One and the same word has several meanings. The liturgically literate person realizes these multiple meanings and knows which meaning should be used in the present and future church.

Let us now briefly look at a second example—the rite of the "breaking of the bread." In the 1570 Missal, the large ("priest's") host was broken during the conclusion of the embolism of the Lord's Prayer. Then with a small particle of the broken host the priest made three signs of the cross over the chalice while saying: "The peace of the Lord be with you always." He then immediately dropped the small particle into the chalice with an accompanying prayer. Then he recited the litany, *Lamb of God*, while striking his breast three times.

An evaluation of this 1570 rite might lead to the conclusion that the important things were the commingling of the particle in the chalice, and the *Lamb of God*. The actual breaking of bread (a biblical action and term) seems to be only preparatory to the commingling, and is discreetly hidden while the priest is reciting the conclusion of the embolism of the *Our Father*.

In the revised Missal, the breaking of bread is supposed to be independent of any other activity. It takes place after the Lord's Prayer, when the sign of peace is finished. While the breaking of the bread takes place, the *Lamb of God* is sung. This hymn should accompany an action, just as the communion hymn accompanies the procession of the assembly to the communion stations. Again, a paradigm-shift has taken place. The biblical action of breaking the bread has been shifted to a rightful place of prominence in the revised

Missal, while the *Lamb of God* has been reduced in prominence from an independent prayer to a hymn accompanying a significant action. Our present paradigm seems to be closer to the biblical models mentioned above. Yet many a priest seems to have misunderstood the deeper importance of the rubrical changes!

Balancing the heritage of the past with the needs of the present is not always easy to do. In our quest for balance, we tend to fall to one side or another too easily. Prayer texts and forms of worship of the first few centuries of the Christian era are not necessarily good or bad solely because of their antiquity. The same holds true of newly composed prayers and orders of worship. Just because they may have been composed by some contemporary Christians does not mean that they will affect other contemporary Christians as well as we might hope. The Lord's Prayer has outlived many a relevant and contemporary prayer. The ultimate criterion should be whether a prayer or rite expresses the age-old faith of Christians and whether it is a help for the local church on its pilgrimage toward heaven. As Dom Botte writes about Eucharistic Prayer II in the revised Missal:

> The anaphora of Hippolytus . . . composed in Rome at the beginning of the third century . . . indeed seems to me to be more worthy of twentieth century people than the rubbish heard today in some churches. The essential thing for a liturgy is not its belonging to one century or to one nation, but the fact that it's Christian, that is, the expression of the faith of the church which belongs to all times.[5]

As we move from the past to the future, as we move toward the next century and the next millennium, we need to *remember* the past, but also *understand* the words we use to describe the past and describe our future. Old paradigms may no longer be valid and perhaps should be refined. New ones may need to be developed. Yet, the danger of anachronism is always present and the danger of wishful thinking to match our desires is also frequently present. Let us hope that the divine power enables us to overcome our foggy vision, to be able to worship our God in the best way possible now and in the future.

NOTES

1. Bernard Botte, O.S.B., *From Silence to Participation: An Insider's View of Liturgical Renewal* (Washington: The Pastoral Press, 1988), p. 1.
2. *Ibid.*, p. 3.
3. Thomas S. Kuhn, *The Structure of Scientific Revolutions* (Chicago: University of Chicago Press, second edition, 1970), p. 10.
4. p. 224, question 9.
5. Botte, *op. cit.*, p. 27.

CHAPTER 5
OVERVIEW

In the *Decree on Ecumenism* of the Second Vatican Council, we are told that "in Catholic doctrine, there exists an order or 'hierarchy' of truths" (ch. 2, n. 11). I would suggest that this principle of doctrine also holds in a modified form for literacy (and, for that matter, in many other realms of human experience, such as in various forms of pedagogy). Hierarchies exist in diverse areas of life. When we learn, we start with fundamental concepts and progress slowly toward other, often more difficult and less frequently used, concepts. Just as with houses, when we build literacy we must start with a solid foundation, then construct the ground level of knowledge, before moving to the second and third stories of specialization.

Since this approach seems to me to have much to offer, I have used it in suggesting a path toward *liturgical literacy*. I have developed *three* lists of terms rather than only one master list as appeared in Hirsch's book. However, to make cross-referencing easier, all terms are listed in proper order in the dictionary chapter (unlike the breakdown into several categories in Hirsch's *Dictionary of Cultural Literacy*). The three lists appear in a somewhat hierarchical order. Starting with the FOUNDATIONAL terms, the reader then progresses to the FLUENCY list, and finally is led to examine the PROFICIENCY words.

Overview

Any categorization of topics will lead to differing opinions as to which topic belongs in which category, and many will probably disagree with the categories into which certain words have been placed. Let me try to explain the reasoning why certain terms appear in one list as opposed to another.

The *Foundations* list consists of a set of ONE HUNDRED core terms which should form the basic vocabulary on which knowledge about present-day liturgy can be built. Take the case of a non-Christian who enters a church or is present for a typical Sunday eucharist or for a Christian wedding or funeral. Which terms permit the most solid foundation for explaining the liturgical rites? Which terms should be included in the minimal word list for liturgical literacy?

The *Contemporary Fluency* list consists of those additional terms which should be known and understood by someone who wishes to read some of the more foundational works and documents on liturgy—or even a version of the basic American Catholic religious education document prior to the Second Vatican Council, the *Baltimore Catechism*. For example, many of the words of this list should be known in order to read the *General Instruction of the Roman Missal*, or to read the two major liturgical documents of the U.S. bishops, *Music in Catholic Worship* and *Environment and Art in Catholic Worship*.

The *Historical and Technical Proficiency* list consists of those additional terms which an individual should know in order to appreciate scholarly (yet still somewhat popular) articles on liturgical questions, articles which may involve technical and subtle points and argumentation. Also included in this list are terms from various other sources, such as historical terms that would enable someone to read a book about the history of liturgy intelligently, or technical terms which would enable someone to know about the more obscure (yet still important) details of a formal liturgy only occasionally held (e.g. the ordination of a bishop).

My hope in arranging the terms into these three lists is that a person might move from one stage of literacy into another, in a logical, though possibly slow, fashion. First graders usually do not start to learn English by reading Shakespeare, yet a person cannot be called literate without knowing about Shakespeare and being able to recognize "To be or not to be . . . ." Just as both "See Dick run" and "The quality of mercy is not strained" are essential to literacy in our modern American culture, so my hope is that the following lists will enable Christians to be liturgically literate.

Yet there are several *caveats*. First and foremost, we must always remember that literacy is more than merely the raw information, or the ability to recognize certain terms. True literacy includes the creative capacity to use the terms toward further growth. It builds on word lists and moves toward wisdom. T. S. Eliot's words are apropos:

> All our knowledge brings us nearer to ignorance
> All our ignorance brings us nearer to death
> But nearness to death, no nearer to God.
> Where is the life we have lost in living?
> Where is the wisdom we have lost in knowledge?
> Where is the knowledge we have lost in information?[1]

In the Christian context, we must also realize that it is the Spirit who gives life (cf. Jn 6:63, "It is the spirit that gives life, while the flesh is of no avail." Mt 26:41, "The spirit is willing, but the flesh is weak"). Intellectual liturgical literacy still might not of itself transform an assembly of spirit-less people unless the things of the head touch the things of the heart. The fruit of liturgical literacy should be a worship which draws one nearer to God and to other Christians.

However, too often the facts that are stored in our brains give rise to a reason which inhibits our growth in the things of God. But, as St. Thomas More says in Robert Bolt's play, *A Man for All Seasons*, "it isn't a matter of reason; finally it's a matter of love."[2]

Secondly, there is a fine line between what is literacy and what is trivia. Is knowing about the Volstead Act trivia or cultural literacy? (It was the 1920 law passed by the U.S. Congress to implement Prohibition, and *is* included in Hirsch's book.) Is knowing Woodrow Wilson's first name trivia or cultural literacy? (It was Thomas, and it is *not* included in Hirsch's book.) Some may wonder why certain words were included in the lists that follow and suggest that they be omitted, but at least these lists are a first step toward further discussion.

Thirdly, some of the terms found in the *Proficiency* list refer to items that are museum pieces or are words that are more jargon than common English. Certain things should remain in museums. We do not need more *burses* and *bugias* cluttering up our contemporary liturgy. Yet unless those who study liturgy seriously know about some of the museum pieces, their perception of where we have come from is defective. Similarly, certain terms may be jargon, but it often helps to know both the jargon and the common term in order to be, as Paul said, "all things to all persons" (1 Cor 9:22). The lists try to include both terms used now and the major terms of years past, so that we may be like the householder of Matthew (13:52) "who brings out of his treasure what is new and what is old."

Lastly, the length of a description does not always bear a direct relation to the importance of the term described. Sometimes a short description of a minor object was not possible, and sometimes a major term has a shorter description because of the abundance of other sources. Those who want to learn more may be able to consult the *New Catholic Encyclopedia* or one of the numerous references given in the Bibliography. The descriptions here are meant as brief overviews, with a "literacy" thrust in them. They try to describe the term and also briefly hint at its present meaning. How well they succeed remains to be seen.

What needs to be remembered in examining the terms is that the worship of God is the ultimate reason why we use these words to begin with. That worship is intimately connected with our love of each other. Being able to recognize the terms in the following lists is useless if we cannot gain wisdom as our liturgies develop and improve in the future. And improved liturgies mean nothing if we fail to improve our relationship with God and our concern for all of God's people.

NOTES

1. "The Rock," Chorus I, in T.S. Eliot, *Collected Poems 1909–1935* (New York: Harcourt, Brace and Co., 1936), p. 179.

2. Robert Bolt, *A Man for All Seasons: A Play in Two Acts* (New York: Random House, 1962), p. 141.

CHAPTER 6
FOUNDATIONS
LIST 1

One Hundred Core Terms

acclamation
Advent
alleluia
altar
Amen
anointing of the sick
ashes
assembly
baptism
bell
bishop
blessing
bow
bread
breaking of the bread
calendar
candle
cantor
celebrant
celebrate
chair, presidential
chalice

choir
Christmas
church
collection
communion
confession
confirmation
congregation
consecration
Creed
cross
cross, sign of the
deacon
Easter
Easter Vigil
eucharist
eucharistic prayer
first reading
font, baptismal
general intercessions
genuflection
Gloria

Good Friday
Gospel
greeting
holy orders
Holy Thursday
homily
hymn
incense
kneeling
lectionary
Lent
liturgy
liturgy of the eucharist
liturgy of the hours
liturgy of the word
Lord's Prayer
marriage
Mass
minister
music
offertory
Ordinary Time
paten
penance
penitential rite
Pentecost
pew
prayers (presidential)

priest
procession
reader
responses
responsorial psalm
ritual
sacrament
sacrifice
sanctuary
season, liturgical
second reading
sermon
server
sign of peace
singing
sitting
standing
stole
Sunday
tabernacle
thanksgiving
usher
vestments
water
water, holy
wine
worship
year, liturgical

CHAPTER 7
CONTEMPORARY FLUENCY LIST 2

ablution bowl
ablutions
absolution
absolution (at the penitential rite)
absolution (in the sacrament of penance)
acolyte
adaptation
adoration, eucharistic
agape
Agnus Dei
alb
altar cloth
ambo
ambry
amice
anamnesis
antependium
antiphon
antiphonal singing
Apostles' Creed
Ash Wednesday
aspergil(-lum)
aspersorium
baptistery
basilica
benediction
Bible
blessed sacrament
boat, incense
Body and Blood of Christ, Solemnity of the
Book of the Gospels
canon
canonical hours
canticle
cassock
catechumen
catechumenate
cathedral
censer
chalice veil
chapel, reservation
chasuble
chrism

chrism Mass
Christ the King, Solemnity
    of
ciborium
cincture
clericalism
closing prayer
collect
colors, liturgical
commemoration
commentator
commingling
commissioning
communal penance service
communion rail
communion service
communion under both
    kinds
community Mass
concelebrant
concelebration
concluding rite
confessional
Confiteor
consecration, supplemental
Constitution on the Sacred
    Liturgy (Vatican II)
conventual Mass
cope
corporal
Corpus Christi
credence table
crosier
cross, pectoral

cross, processional
crucifix
cruet
cup
dalmatic
dance, liturgical
dedication of churches
dismissal
doxology
drama, liturgical
dulia
Easter candle
elect
elements
elevation
embolism
epiclesis
Epiphany
eulogy
evening prayer
exclusive language
exposition of the blessed
    sacrament
Exsúltet
fast, Easter (paschal)
fast, eucharistic
fast, Friday
fast, lenten
fast, pre-baptismal
fasting
feast
feasts
final commendation
finger towel

Fluency

form
form, declarative
form, deprecative
form, indicative
form, invocative
forms (literary) of blessings, absolutions, etc.
Forty Hours
fraction rite
funeral
funeral Mass
gesture
godparent
gospel acclamation
gospel procession
gradual
greeter
Gregorian chant
gremial
Hail Mary
hands, extending (imposition/laying on) of
healing, sacraments of
hierarchy
Holy Family, Feast of
holy, holy, holy
holy week
hospitality, minister of
host
humeral veil
hyperdulia
icon
immersion, baptism by

inclusive language
initiation, sacraments of
institution (of ministers)
institution narrative
intercessions, eucharistic prayer
intercommunion
intinction
introductory rites
introit
kiss
kneeler
Kyrie
laity, priesthood of the
Lamb of God
language, Latin
language, liturgical
language, sexist
language, vernacular
Last Supper
latria
lauds
lectern
lectio continua
lector
lights, processional
litany
liturgical movement
liturgy committee
Lord
Lord's Day
Lord's Supper
lunette
mandatum

Marian devotions
Marian month
martyr
Mass of Christian burial
Mass of the Resurrection
master of ceremonies
matrimony
matter
May, month of
meal
memorial
memorial acclamation
metaphor
minister, eucharistic
minister, extraordinary
minister, ordinary
minister, special
minister to the sick
Missal, Roman
missalette
miter
mixed chalice
monstrance
morning prayer
musician
mystagogical catechesis
mystagogy
mystery
narthex
nave
neophyte
Nicene Creed
night prayer
novena

nuptial blessing
nuptial Mass
objects, liturgical
obligation, holy day of
octave
offering
offering, mass
oil of the catechumens
oil of the sick
opening prayer
orans
ordinary of the mass
ordination
ordo
pall, chalice
pall, funeral
pallium
palms
paraliturgy
Pascha
paschal candle
paschal mystery
Passion [Palm] Sunday
Passover
planner
plate
pontifical
prayer after communion
prayer over the gifts
prayer over the people
prayers of the faithful
preaching
predella
preface

Fluency

preparation of the altar and gifts
presbyter
presbyterium
presider
prie-dieu
procession with the gifts
profession of faith
profession, religious
proper of the mass
psalm
pulpit
purification
purificator
pyx
R.C.I.A.
reconciliation
reconciliation room (chapel)
relics, saints'
repose, altar of
reservation, eucharistic
ring, bishop's
ring, wedding
rite
rite of Christian initiation of adults
rosary
rubric
sabbath
sacramental
sacramentary
sacrarium
Sacred Heart, Solemnity of the
sacristy
saints
salt
sanctorale
sanctuary light (candle / lamp)
Sanctus
scrutiny
sequence
serve
service
sick, pastoral care of the
sign
silence
solemn blessing
solemnity
space, liturgical
sponsor
spoon, incense
stations of the cross
statues
stipend
stock, holy oil
stole fee
stoup, holy water
surplice
symbol
symbols, liturgical
tabernacle veil
table
temporale
throne, bishop's
thurible
thurifer

time
tract
tradition
Transfiguration, Feast of the
transubstantiation
Tridentine Mass
triduum, Easter (paschal / sacred)
Trinity, Solemnity of the Holy
veil
verse before the Gospel

vespers
vestibule
viaticum
vigil
vocation, sacraments of
votive candles
votive Mass
washing of feet
washing of hands
word of God
zucchetto

CHAPTER 8
HISTORICAL AND TECHNICAL PROFICIENCY LIST 3

75
215
1054
1517
1570
1832
1909
1947
1963
1970
Abba
absolution (in the funeral liturgy)
abstinence
accidents
accommodation
acculturation
Addai and Mari
aesthetic
affective
affusion, baptism by

Alcuin
aliturgical day
allegorization
allegory
altar stone
Ambrose of Milan
analogy
anaphora
antidoron
antimension
apocalyptic
appropriation
apse
architecture, liturgical
archpriest
art, liturgical
asperges
Augustine of Hippo
baldachino
Basil of Caesarea
Beauduin, Lambert

Benedict
berakah
bidding prayers
biretta
birkat ha-mazon
Book of Blessings
Botte, Bernard
Bouyer, Louis
breviary
bugia
burse
Byzantine Christianity
Byzantine Rite
Campbell, Joseph
Candlemas
canopy
Casel, Odo
cathedra
Ceremonial of Bishops
chancel
chrismation
christology
churching
Common Prayer, Book of
compline
Congregation for Divine Worship
conopaeum
consecration of bishops
consecration of churches
consent
Consilium
consubstantiation
covenant service
Cranmer, Thomas
cuffs
cult
cultural adaptation
Cyril of Alexandria
Cyril of Jerusalem
Daniélou, Jean
deaconess
Didache
Diekmann, Godfrey
Dies Irae
diptychs
Directory for Masses with Children
divine office
divine office, cathedral form
divine office, monastic form
Dix, Gregory
Douglas, Mary
ecclesiology
economy
Egeria
Eliade, Mircea
Ellard, Gerald
ember days
energy
enlightenment, period of
Environment and Art in Catholic Worship
epistle
epistle side
epitrachelion
euchology
eulogia

evangelarium
ex opere operantis
ex opere operato
exorcism
exorcist
extreme unction
faith and order
faldstool
fanon
feria
fermentum
fibula
First Friday
First Saturday
flabella
folded chasuble
frontal
Gelineau, Joseph
General Instruction of the Liturgy of the Hours
General Instruction of the Roman Missal
gloves, liturgical
gospel side
grail psalms
Great Entrance
Gregory the Great
Guardini, Romano
Guéranger, Prosper
Hebrew scriptures
high church
high Mass
Hippolytus
iconastasis

inculturation
indulgence
Jansenism
Jerome
John XXIII, Pope
John Chrysostom
Jungmann, Josef Andreas
Justin
kenosis
kiss of peace
koinonia
lamb
lappets
Last Gospel
last rites
lavábo
Lavanaux, Maurice
leonine prayers (after Mass)
lex orandi, lex credendi
Liber Usualis
Liturgical Music Today
low church
low Mass
Low Sunday
Luther, Martin
Lutheran Book of Worship
major orders
maniple
Maria Laach
Mass of the catechumens
Mass of the faithful
Mass of the Pre-sanctified
Maundy Thursday
McManus, Frederick

Mediator Dei
methodism
Michel, Virgil
mimesis
minor orders
missa pro populo
morse
Music in Catholic Worship
must
myth
narrative
ombrellino
omophorion
orarion
orthodoxy
orthopraxis
ostensorium
Otto, Rudolf
panniculus
Parsch, Pius
passiontide
Paul VI, Pope
phelon(ion)
Phos Hilaron
porter
prayers at the foot of the altar
preces
preconium
preparer
presbyterianism
prime
progressive solemnity
prosphora

prothesis
quinceanera
Quinquagesima Sunday
reenactment
reformation
reformed liturgy
reliquary
requiem Mass
reredos
res tantum
responsory
ripidion
Ritual, Roman
rogation days
Roman Rite
rood screen
sacramentum et res
sacramentum tantum
Sacrosanctum Concilium
Schmemann, Alexander
secret
secretarium
sedia gestatoria
Septuagesima Sunday
Serapion
Sexagesima Sunday
skull cap
solemn annual exposition
solemn Mass
Solesmes
spoon for communion
spoon for water
stational Mass
straw, liturgical

Proficiency

subdeacon
substance
synaxis
synergy
Te Deum
tenebrae
Theodore of Mopsuestia
theophany
theotokos
tiara
tonsure

transfinalization
transignification
transmutation
trisagion
tunic
Turner, Victor
vimpa
Whitsunday
zikkaron
zone

CHAPTER 9
THE DICTIONARY

NOTES: The number in parentheses after each entry is the list number in which the entry appears.

In the explanations, a reference to another pertinent word in the dictionary is indicated by **boldface type**, although not every possible cross-reference is so indicated. A self-reference is indicated by *italics*, and other important concepts are also sometimes emphasized by *italics*.

Where a reference to a major document is possible, it occurs after the description part of each entry. The three common abbreviations used are: **GIRM** for the *General Instruction of the Roman Missal*, **LM** for the *Introduction to the Lectionary for Mass* (1981 text), **EACW** for *Environment and Art in Catholic Worship*. If a *confer* is indicated in the reference, the document in question further explains the concept, but does not use the exact word.

75 (3) – Approximate year of the editing of the **Didache**, a document containing some of the earliest written accounts of Christian liturgies.

215 (3) – Approximate year of the writing of the *Apostolic Tradition* of **Hippolytus**, a document containing numerous liturgies, along with the first complete text of a eucharistic prayer and of ordination prayers.

1054 (3) – The date of the Great Schism, which separated the Orthodox east from the Catholic west. This schism also for centuries isolated the **Byzantine** style of liturgical rites from the Roman style.

1517 (3) – The year when **Martin Luther**, on October 31, posted his 95 theses on the church door in Wittenberg, Germany. It is considered to be the start of the Protestant Reformation and the starting point for the liturgical reforms which were undertaken at that time (e.g. vernacular liturgies).

1570 (3) – The year of the promulgation by Pope Pius V of the **Roman Missal** that was revised at the order of the Council of Trent. This version of the Missal is frequently called the *Tridentine Missal* and the order of Mass found in it is often referred to as the *Tridentine Mass*. It was in use, with minor changes, until the Missal promulgated by Pope Paul VI in 1970.

1832 (3) – The year of the re-founding of the Benedictine Abbey at **Solesmes**. This date is also considered by some as the beginning of the **liturgical movement**.

1909 (3) – The year of Dom **Lambert Beauduin's** address at the National Congress of Catholic Works held in Malines, Belgium. This date is also considered by many as the beginning of the contemporary phase of the **liturgical movement**.

1947 (3) – The date of the encyclical **Mediator Dei** by Pope Pius XII which gave papal support to the **liturgical movement**.

1963 (3) – The date of the promulgation of the first decree by the Second Vatican Council, the **Constitution on the Sacred Liturgy, Sacrosanctum Concilium**.

1970 (3) – The date of the promulgation by Pope Paul VI of the **Roman Missal** that was revised at the order of the Second Vatican Council. The Order of Mass and the Lectionary were published in 1969, but the complete Missal, with the presidential prayers and revised rites of Holy Week, did not appear until 1970.

ABBA (3) – Hebrew endearment form of the word for *father*, possibly translated as *daddy*, or *papa*. It was used by Jesus (Mk 14:36) and by Paul (Gal 4:6) in referring to God. Christian liturgical tradition has continued the use of the title "Father," as appropriate in liturgical prayer.

ABLUTION BOWL (2) – The bowl of water, normally covered, frequently found near the **tabernacle**. It was explicitly mentioned in the Rite for Distributing Communion Outside of Mass found in the old **Roman Ritual**, which required a priest to purify the "fingers which touched the sacrament." The revised rite merely states that the minister "may" wash his or her "hands" after communion is distributed and does not describe how this is done, but the use of the *ablution bowl* is still widespread.

ABLUTIONS (2) – An older term for the cleansing of vessels after communion, particularly of the chalice. The Tridentine Missal directed the priest to purify the chalice himself, using both wine and water. This cleansing is now usually called the **purifications**. (cf. GIRM 237–239)

ABSOLUTION (2) – A text declaring or requesting from God the forgiveness of sins. (See the next three entries.)

ABSOLUTION (in the funeral liturgy) (3) – The title given to the prayers recited over the coffin at the end of a funeral Mass before these rites were revised in 1969. The revised rites now call this sequence of prayers the **final commendation**.

ABSOLUTION (at the penitential rite) (2) – The concluding statement of the **penitential rite** at Mass ("May almighty God have mercy on us, forgive us our sins, . . . ") is called an **absolution**. (GIRM 29)

ABSOLUTION (in the sacrament of penance) (2) – The solemn declaration of the priest ("God, the Father of mercies, . . . I absolve you . . . ") used in the sacrament of **penance** is called an **absolution** and constitutes the **form** of the sacrament. It is pronounced while the priest extends his **hands** (or at least his right hand) over the head of the penitent.

ABSTINENCE (3) – Refraining from eating a certain type of food. Roman Catholic law prescribes that, in general, Fridays are days of abstinence from meat, a practice which can be adapted by the national conference of bishops (canon 1251). This is commonly called the **Friday fast**. **Byzantine Rite** Christians practice abstinence from dairy products as well on certain penitential days. *Abstinence* is sometimes called **fasting** and, in fact, can be considered a specific form of it. Before revisions of the **Calendar** and the laws of fasting, certain days were also designated days of *partial abstinence* in which meat could be eaten only at the principal meal.

ACCIDENTS (3) – External appearances of physical matter. It is a classical philosophical term used in distinction to **substance**. This distinction provides the basis for the explanation of the change in the eucharistic elements which is called **transubstantiation**.

ACCLAMATION (1) – A shout (of joy) by the assembly during worship. Certain responses of the assembly are classified as *acclamations*, as opposed to hymns, responses, or other literary forms. E.g. **Amen** is an *acclamation* while the **Gloria** is a hymn, and the **Agnus Dei** is a series of invocations in the style of a **litany**. (GIRM 15; Music in Catholic Worship 53)

ACCOMMODATION (3) – (Minor) modifications that the minister may make in a rite because of circumstances. Technically, a minister may only make *accommodations* in a rite rather than **adaptations**, although the English translations of the Latin rubrics frequently render both Latin terms as *adaptation*.

ACCULTURATION (3) – The process of modifying a liturgical rite by introducing elements of the local culture into it. For example, *acculturation* will take the established (European) format, and modify certain aspects of it by substituting a local cultural element for the original (European) element, e.g., the substitution of a bow for a genuflection, or a solemn touch for a liturgical kiss. This is sometimes contrasted to the process of **inculturation**.

ACOLYTE (2) – The liturgical minister charged with assisting the presiding priest and deacon in the sanctuary. Although the title is frequently applied to any altar **server**, an *acolyte* is blessed and commissioned for his ministry through a special rite of **institution**. Formerly, it was regarded as one of the **minor orders**. (GIRM 65, 142–147)

ADAPTATION (2) – Major modifications in a rite. Any such modifications must be approved by the national conference of bishops for significant pastoral benefits (e.g. for cultural reasons). (GIRM 325)

ADDAI and MARI (3) – The title of an old Nestorian **anaphora** is that of the "Apostles Addai and Mari," who were, by legend, two of the Lord's 72 disciples. This **eucharistic prayer** is unique in that, in most ancient manuscripts, it lacks the **institution narrative** containing the words of Christ. Dom **Bernard Botte** argued that the original must have contained such a narrative, but his argument has been disputed by other scholars.

ADORATION, EUCHARISTIC (2) – The traditional Catholic belief that the consecrated eucharistic elements are the Lord's body and blood, and that this reality remains after the conclusion of the celebration of the eucharist, has led to the practice of prayer before the sacrament reserved in a **tabernacle**, and the adoration of Christ's presence in the elements. (GIRM 276)

ADVENT (1) – The preparation period before **Christmas**, which starts on the fourth Sunday before Christmas. It is a **season** of waiting and spiritual preparation, and only secondarily a time of penance. The first Sunday of Advent is considered to be the beginning of the Church's **liturgical year** according to the Roman Calendar.

AESTHETIC (3) – The aspect or quality of something that pertains to a sense of beauty.

AFFECTIVE (3) – Pertaining to love and the emotions.

AFFUSION, BAPTISM BY (3) – The method of administering baptism by which the minister pours water over the head of the candidate while pronouncing the traditional formula. This is a standard (and convenient) way of administering the sacrament in the west, although baptism by **immersion** is to be preferred because of its fuller symbolism.

AGAPE (2) – Greek word for *love*, especially a love of God. It is frequently used to denote a "love-feast" sometimes held in connection with or following a eucharistic celebration, but not a sacrament itself. Scholars debate whether the ritual described in the **Didache** (ch. 9) is a **eucharist** or an *agape* or whether the Christians of the first two centuries would have made a distinction.

AGNUS DEI (2) – Latin for *Lamb of God*. It usually refers to the litany of invocations prescribed to be sung during the **breaking of the bread**. Although commonly sung as a whole, the assembly need only sing the final responses, "have mercy on us / grant us peace." Although usually consisting of only three invocations, it may be repeated as long as needed, until the bread is broken and the cups are prepared for communion. (GIRM 56e)

ALB (2) – A term derived from the Latin word for *white* (*albus*), which refers to a floor-length white or natural tan colored robe. The *alb* is now considered the preferred common **vestment** for all ministers, from bishop to server. Ordained ministers wear **stoles** and other outer garments over the alb. (GIRM 298)

ALCUIN (735–604) (3) – British deacon and friend of Charlemagne. He was highly influential in reforming the liturgy of his era. He reordered the Roman baptismal rite and lectionary, among other achievements.

ALITURGICAL DAY (3) – A day on which the eucharistic liturgy is *not* celebrated. In the Roman Rite, Good Friday and Holy Saturday are aliturgical days (even though communion is distributed on Friday). In the Byzantine Rite, Monday through Friday of Lenten weeks are aliturgical (although a Liturgy of the **Pre-Sanctified** is celebrated on Wednesdays and Fridays). In the Ambrosian Rite (Milan, Italy), Fridays of Lent are aliturgical.

ALLEGORIZATION (3) – The process of attaching allegorical meanings, especially to religious texts or liturgical rites.

ALLEGORY (3) – A sustained metaphor, a literary device in which the external appearance clothes the presumed real, but hidden, meaning. This was a standard method of explaining liturgical rites, especially when the historical origins were unknown. For example, the allegorical interpretation of placing the priest's paten under the corporal in the Tridentine Mass was that it signified the flight of the apostles at the arrest of Jesus.

ALLELUIA (1) – Hebrew for *Praise Yah(-weh)*, i.e., *Praise the Lord*. It is used especially during Easter time, and omitted during Lent. It forms a special hymn sung by all to prepare for the gospel reading (and accompany the formal procession before the gospel). If the *alleluia* before the gospel cannot be sung, it is to be omitted rather than merely being recited. (LM 23; GIRM 37)

ALTAR (1) – A wooden or stone table on which bread and wine are placed for the **liturgy of the eucharist**. It is the basic symbol of Christ in a church building. Even though it is a focal point for the eucharistic celebration, it need not be the mathematical center of the **sanctuary**. The other two focal points in the sanctuary are the **ambo** and the **presidential chair**. (GIRM 259; EACW 71–73)

ALTAR CLOTH (2) – The cloth used to cover the altar during the celebration of Mass. In the Tridentine Missal, three white cloths were prescribed, the top-most being long enough to extend down the sides of the altar. Now only one is required, and it need not be white, nor be on the altar outside the time of Mass. (GIRM 268)

ALTAR STONE (3) – The Tridentine Missal demanded that Mass be celebrated on an altar solemnly consecrated by a bishop. Such an altar was supposed to have the *mensa* (i.e., top) be of stone with five crosses carved into it and a place for **relics** of martyrs to be entombed. The base of such an altar had to be in the ground as well. Relatively few such altars existed. In lieu of such a solemn consecration, most altars had an *altar stone*, which was about an inch thick and about 10 inches square. This stone was solemnly consecrated and had the five carved crosses and the relics. If Mass was to be said outside a sacred place, an altar stone had to be used. In the Byzantine Rite, a special cloth, the **antimension**, served the same purpose, having been solemnly blessed by a bishop and containing relics of saints. With permission, Roman Rite priests could occasionally use a Byzantine antimension in lieu of a Roman altar stone. Such a stone is no longer required. (cf. GIRM 265)

AMBO (2) – A term derived from a Greek word for *raised place*. It now usually refers to the place (and structure) at which *all* the Scripture readings are proclaimed during a liturgy. There should be only one *ambo* for reading from Scripture, used by all readers, whether lay or ordained. Non-scriptural announcements should be done at another place, along with the introductory and concluding rites of the Mass. Technically, the ambo is a place, originally in the middle of the **nave**, and (usually) at the ambo is a stand (i.e. **lectern** or **pulpit**) to hold the book. However, the reading stand is also termed the *ambo* as well. Together with the **altar** and the **presidential chair**, the ambo is a focal point in the sanctuary. (GIRM 272; EACW 74)

AMBROSE OF MILAN (c. 339–397) (3) – Bishop of Milan, chosen by popular acclamation in 374 to be bishop even though he was the civil governor and still a catechumen. He baptized **St. Augustine,** and was the first to make extensive use of hymns in worship. In his treatise *De sacramentis*, there are preserved large sections of a eucharistic prayer, very similar to the Roman canon, along with a description of the rite of receiving communion which includes the formula "The body of Christ" and the response "Amen." (Introduction to GIRM 8)

AMBRY (2) – A wall safe, usually housing the Holy Oils, that is, the **chrism,** the **oil of the sick,** and the **oil of the catechumens.** Sometimes the eucharistic **tabernacle** is in the form of an *ambry*. It is also spelled *aumbry*.

AMEN (1) – A concluding response to prayer texts or formulas which indicates agreement. It is a Hebrew word meaning *So be it*, and is used by the assembly to indicate agreement with the prayers proclaimed by the presiding minister at a worship service. The "great" Amen is the concluding acclamation to the **eucharistic prayer.**

AMICE (2) – A (linen) cloth, approximately two feet by three feet in size, with tie ribbons. It is a **vestment** worn under the **alb.** The *amice* is draped over the shoulders and is usually tucked around the collar to protect the alb and to cover the shirt of the minister. Its use was prescribed by the Tridentine Missal, but is now optional. (GIRM 298)

ANALOGY (3) – A comparison of a similar quality of two different things to each other. This is done to gain a better understanding of one of the two things. For example, we try to understand the nature of three "persons" in God by analogy to the concept of human persons.

ANAMNESIS (2) – *Anamnesis*, 'Ανάμνησις, a Greek word, derived from the verb "remember." As mentioned in chapter 2, in the Christian liturgical context *anamnesis* refers to "active" remembrance. The present is brought into intimate contact with the past, and the past with the present. This Greek word tries to capture what the Hebrew word **zikkaron** means. *Anamnesis* is the word used in Christ's command: "Do this in *memory* of me"(Lk 22:19). As a liturgical term, it sometimes refers to any act of remembering that gives context to the present liturgical celebration. It can specifically be used to refer to the section of the **eucharistic prayer** following the institution narrative in which the presiding priest explicitly remembers Christ's death and resurrection while making a statement of **offering**. Sometimes, this *remembering* aspect of liturgy is contrasted with the invocation or petition aspect, often termed the **epiclesis**. Thus, *remembering* leads to *request*. (GIRM 55e)

ANAPHORA (3) – Greek term used for the **eucharistic prayer**. The word is derived from the verb for *offer*.

ANOINTING OF THE SICK (1) – The sacrament of healing that may be given to seriously ill individuals and which finds its biblical basis in James 5:14. Those who are ill are anointed with the specially blessed **oil of the sick**. It may be conferred during Mass. Formerly, this sacrament was called **extreme unction**.

ANTEPENDIUM (2) – A partial hanging, usually matching the liturgical color, that covers the front of the **ambo** or of the **altar**.

ANTIDORON (3) – Pieces of bread distributed at the end of a **Byzantine Rite** eucharistic liturgy. It consists of the left-over pieces of bread from which particles were taken for the consecration and communion. Originally given to non-communicants, it is now given to all in the church as a sign of fellowship. A corresponding custom in the Roman Rite, especially in French-speaking areas, was the distribution of non-consecrated bread called **eulogia**.

ANTIMENSION (3) – A special cloth used in the Byzantine Rite on which the burial of Christ is depicted and into which relics have been sewed. The *antimension* functions both as an **altar stone** and as a **corporal** and is consecrated by a bishop who signs it.

ANTIPHON (2) – A short refrain, frequently a verse of a psalm, that is suggested as a repeated congregational response to a psalm used during a liturgy, for example, as the entrance song or the communion song. (GIRM 26, 56i)

ANTIPHONAL SINGING (2) – The type of singing in which a soloist sings the verses of a hymn (psalm), while the assembly sings merely a brief antiphon between the verses. This seems to be the more ancient form of liturgical singing. The *chorale* form in which the assembly sings all the text of the hymn is a more recent development in the Roman Church.

APOCALYPTIC (3) – Referring to the type of image or vision portrayed in the *Apocalypse*, i.e. the book of

The Dictionary

Revelation in the Bible. It is often associated with images of the end of the world and visions of the fulfillment of all creation in a new heaven and a new earth (Rev 21:1). Many liturgical images (e.g. the Lamb, the altar, the incense) are *apocalyptic* in origin.

APOSTLES' CREED (2) – A common form of the **profession of faith**, shorter than the **Nicene Creed**, that is associated with baptism (at which it usually is found in a question and answer form). It may be used at children's Masses in lieu of the Nicene Creed, or in certain countries that possess an indult (e.g. Canada, Italy).

APPROPRIATION (3) – The custom of assigning, because of limitations of mind and language, to one person qualities that are shared by others. For example, the presiding priest is frequently termed the "celebrant" even though every member of the assembly is truly a "celebrant" of the liturgy.

APSE (3) – The vaulted, semi-circular or polygonal end of the **sanctuary** or **chancel**.

ARCHITECTURE, LITURGICAL (3) – The form of architecture that integrates the best of contemporary art forms and building designs with the demands of the revised liturgy. Not every architectural design is properly liturgical for contemporary worship. Old churches and modern theaters both may be unsuitable models for contemporary worship spaces. Many authors emphasize that modern *liturgical architecture* should help to emphasize the central role of the **assembly** at any liturgy, and help prevent those present from being mere spectators as if at a movie or a concert. The building for worship must be seen as a house for God's *people*, and it should help the worship taking place become the action of the entire assembly. General principles along with specific requirements are described in GIRM, Chapter V (253–280), and in EACW. (cf. EACW 28)

ARCHPRIEST (3) – The senior assistant priest at a bishop's Mass or the Mass of a newly-ordained was frequently called an *archpriest*.

ART, LITURGICAL (3) – An art form that serves the liturgy being celebrated, whether visually, aurally, or otherwise. As with **liturgical architecture**, *liturgical art* must not merely copy the religious models of centuries ago nor the contemporary art of the common culture. General principles along with specific requirements are described in GIRM, Chapter VI (287–295, 311–312), and in EACW.

ASH WEDNESDAY (2) – The first day of **Lent** in the Roman Rite, celebrated during the seventh week before **Easter**, on which **ashes** are blessed and distributed. (GIRM 316a, 330)

ASHES (1) – Used as a sign of repentance on **Ash Wednesday**. They are derived from the **palms** or other branches blessed the previous year on **Passion [Palm] Sunday**. Individuals are signed with the ashes on the forehead (in the form of a cross), or the ashes may be sprinkled on the top of a person's head.

ASPERGES (3) – A rite of sprinkling **holy water** on the assembly that used to precede the formal start of the high Mass or the solemn Mass of the Tridentine Missal. The water was previously blessed, and the sprinkling was accompanied by the verse *Asperges me* ("You will sprinkle me") or, during the Easter season, the verse *Vidi Aquam* ("I saw water"). This rite was revised and incorporated into the 1970 Missal as an alternative to the **penitential rite** on Sundays.

ASPERGIL(-LUM) (2) – The sprinkler used to sprinkle **holy water**.

ASPERSORIUM (2) – The small bucket or vessel that holds **holy water** and can be carried for sprinkling the assembly. Sometimes the sprinkler (*aspergil*) is called the *aspersorium* as well.

ASSEMBLY (1) – The people gathered together for divine worship, often called the **congregation**. Because of the statement of Christ, "Where two or three are gathered in my name, there I am in their midst" (Mt 18:20), and the statement of St. Paul, "You are the body of Christ" (1 Cor 12:27), the *assembly* is seen as the basic symbol of Christ at a liturgical action. Contemporary liturgical writers emphasize that it is the *assembly* as a whole that celebrates the liturgy under the leadership of a priest (who is himself a member of the assembly). Anything that causes members of the assembly to be passive spectators, or causes them to see themselves as isolated individuals rather than the unified body of Christ, or causes them to think that the liturgy is the work of the ministers rather than the action of the assembly, is contrary to the spirit of the renewed liturgy. The central role of the assembly thus influences (among other things) liturgical **architecture**. (GIRM 7; EACW 11, 29)

AUGUSTINE OF HIPPO (354–430) (3) – Son of St. Monica, he was baptized by St. **Ambrose** later in life and still later became bishop of Hippo. Many sacramental and liturgical themes run through his writings. He upheld the validity of baptisms administered by heretics (against the Donatists), and gave an early definition of a sacrament: *accedit verbum ad elementum et fit sacramentum* ("the word is joined to the element and a sacrament is constituted") (*Super Joann.* LXXX on 15:3, Migne's *Patrologia Latina* 35:1840).

BALDACHINO (3) – The dome-like canopy structure that is frequently built over the major altar, often supported by four or more pillars. Technically, it should be called a baldachino only if the canopy is cloth; otherwise it is known as a **ciborium**. There are variant spellings.

BAPTISM (1) – The **sacrament** bestowed by **immersion** in water or by the pouring of water over the head (a method called **affusion**). This washing with water is accompanied by a formula (i.e., **form**) based on the text found at the end of Matthew's gospel (Mt 28:19), e.g., "I baptize you in the name of the Father, and of the Son, and of the Holy Spirit" (for the Roman Rite) or "The servant of God is baptized in the name of the Father, and of the Son, and of the Holy Spirit" (for the Byzantine Rite). The same individual acting as the minister must help immerse the candidate (or pour the water) and pronounce the form. *Baptism* is the first and foundational Christian sacrament, a prerequisite for receiving the **eucharist**. By baptism, an individual becomes one of the "faithful" and participates in the **priesthood of the laity**. Baptism is most properly administered to adults during the **Easter Vigil**. Occasionally, the baptism of infants may occur during Sunday Mass. (GIRM 3)

BAPTISTERY (2) – A separate section of the church building or even a separate building where the baptismal **font** is located and where baptisms are performed. (EACW 76–77)

BASIL OF CAESAREA (c. 330–379) (3) – Called the "Great," bishop of Caesarea. He is credited as being the author of one of the two principal liturgies used in the **Byzantine Rite**, although this authorship is probably not historically exact. Some of the phrases of the eucharistic prayer of the Liturgy of Basil have parallels in his writings.

BASILICA (2) – A title of honor given by the pope to certain churches. A *basilica* outside of Rome usually enshrines two special papal insignia that are signs of its status—the *tintinnabulum*, a special bell once carried in papal processions, and the gold and blue papal *ombellino* (umbrella). As a style of architecture, the ancient Roman *basilica* was a rectangular public building with a wide **nave**, an **apse** at one end, and with colonnaded side aisles.

BEAUDUIN, LAMBERT (1873–1960) (3) – Belgian Benedictine monk and founder of the bi-ritual monastery of Chevetogne. He was also founding editor of the journal *Questions Liturgiques*, and one of the founders of the Centre de Pastorale Liturgique in Paris. Around 1909,

Beauduin reportedly said in a class he was teaching, "I've just realized that the liturgy is the center of the piety of the church!" His address in **1909** at the National Congress of Catholic Works in Malines, Belgium is seen by many as the birth of the modern **Liturgical Movement**.

BELL (1) – *Bells* have been commonly associated with churches for centuries. The larger church bells, housed in a steeple, frequently serve as a call to worship, especially when used to announce the time for the recitation of the *Angelus* prayer at 6 am, noon, and 6 pm. A special bell is sometimes tolled at funerals. There is a solemn blessing for such bells in the **Book of Blessings**. In the course of the Mass, if it is customary, a small hand bell may be rung during the **eucharistic prayer** before the institution narrative, and when the bread and cup are shown to the assembly. The Missal prescribes that the church bells be rung during the **Gloria** of the Mass of the Lord's Supper on **Holy Thursday** and then remain silent until the *Gloria* of the **Easter Vigil**. (GIRM 109)

BENEDICT (480–546) (3) – Founder of Benedictine monasticism and considered to be the father of western monasticism. The *Rule of St. Benedict* states: "Let nothing be preferred to the Work of God" (43:3), referring to the **liturgy of the hours**. The practice of *lectio divina*, an imbibing of and reflection on the word of God, was also encouraged by him.

BENEDICTION (2) – A rite that includes the solemn blessing (*benediction* strictly speaking) with the **blessed sacrament** contained either in the **ciborium** of reservation, or in a **monstrance**. Present liturgical regulations demand the inclusion of scriptural readings, hymns, and silence as part of the ceremony and forbid the mere **exposition** of the eucharist solely for the purpose of the blessing.

BERAKAH (3) – (Plural: *berakoth*) A Hebrew prayer form that usually begins with "Blessed are you, Lord our God, King of the universe." This is the basic style of the Hebrew grace after meals, the **birkat ha-mazon**, which seems to be the ancestor of the Christian **eucharistic prayer**.

BIBLE (2) – The fundamental book of religious writings of the Judeo-Christian tradition. The psalms from the Hebrew section of the *Bible* were the original hymnal for both Jewish and Christian worship. Proclamations of sections from the Bible usually form a significant part of every worship service. (GIRM 34)

BIDDING PRAYERS (3) – An older name, particularly used in Great Britain, for the **general intercessions**.

BIRETTA (3) – A clerical hat with three or four upward pointed semi-circles and frequently with a center pompom. It is a cousin to the American academic mortarboard, and the Tridentine Missal prescribed that the clergy wear a *biretta* to and from the sanctuary for Mass and while seated during the liturgy.

BIRKAT HA-MAZON (3) – The Hebrew name for grace after meals. This prayer has a **berakah** form with a three-fold structure, the first part being a blessing of God, the second part being a thanksgiving, and the third part being an intercession. For some feasts, the prayer could be expanded to include a commemoration of the event being celebrated. Most scholars consider the *birkat ha-mazon* to be the immediate ancestor of the Christian **eucharistic prayer**.

BISHOP (1) – The standard English word used to translate the Greek biblical term *episkopos*, a word meaning *over-seer* or *supervisor*. It is considered the final of the three grades of special ministry that may be received through the sacrament of **holy orders**. The bishop heads the local community of Christians in the territorial area called a diocese. Only a bishop may administer the sacrament of holy orders. In the Roman Rite, he normally also administers the sacrament of **confirmation**. Liturgies presided over by a bishop are seen as the ideal form of worship—the head of the local church, surrounded by his assistant ministers, leading the assembled believers in prayer. (GIRM 59)

BLESSED SACRAMENT (2) – The name commonly used to refer to the eucharistic elements of bread and wine after consecration. When reserved in a **tabernacle**, it is the focus of **eucharistic adoration** outside of Mass. (See the entry for **eucharistic reservation** below.)

BLESSING (1) – Any prayer that praises and thanks God. In particular, *blessing* describes those prayers in which God is blessed because of some person or object, and thus the individual or the object is seen to have become specially dedicated or sanctified because of the prayer of faith. Traditionally, many such *blessing* prayers explicitly call God's favor upon a person or object, and for many people, a *blessing* is primarily the conferring of God's power on a person or object which is thus considered blessed. Worship services usually conclude with a blessing pronounced over the assembly by the presiding minister. Such a concluding blessing may be expanded by the use of a **prayer over the people** or a triple **solemn blessing**. (GIRM 57) (See **Book of Blessings** below.)

BOAT, INCENSE (2) – The vessel used to contain incense grains, before these are burnt in a **censer**.

BODY AND BLOOD OF CHRIST, SOLEMNITY OF THE (2) – A solemnity occurring on the second Thursday after Pentecost. In many countries (e.g., the United States and Canada) its observance is transferred to the following Sunday. In some countries, it is marked by a solemn procession with the **blessed sacrament**. It was formerly called **Corpus Christi**.

BOOK OF BLESSINGS (3) – The name given to the section of the revised **Roman Ritual** that contains **blessings** for various occasions. It was published in Latin in 1984. Some of these blessings (e.g. for a wedding anniversary) may be given during the celebration of Mass, and others are more appropriately invoked in a special celebration (e.g. for an engaged couple). In a number of cases, the rubrics specify a lay minister for certain blessings (e.g. *parents* when blessing their children).

BOOK OF THE GOSPELS (2) – A special book containing the passages from the four gospels assigned to be proclaimed at Mass. It may be carried in the entrance procession and placed on the altar during the liturgy of the word. It is presented to deacons at their ordination, and held over the heads of bishops at their ordination. (GIRM 82d, 128, 232)

BOTTE, BERNARD (1893–1980) (3) – Belgian Benedictine liturgist. He is known for his historical studies of ancient liturgical texts and published critical editions of numerous such texts. He is also known for his argument about the original existence of an institution narrative in the anaphora of Sts. **Addai and Mari**, even though such a narrative does not exist in any known manuscript. He was highly influential in the liturgical renewal centers of Paris, and was a key figure in the revision of the rites of ordination. He also participated in the 1960's revision of the Mass as a consultor to the **Consilium**.

BOUYER, LOUIS (b. 1913) (3) – French Oratorian liturgist. He authored numerous books among which are: *Rite and Man: Natural Sacredness and Christian Liturgy; Liturgical Piety; Eucharist: Theology and Spirituality of the Eucharistic Prayer.*

BOW (1) – An inclination of the upper half of the body or of the head. It is a sign of respect for certain individuals and sacred objects. The ministers normally make a bow toward the altar at the beginning and end of Mass, and when certain prayers are said. Some monasteries use a *bow* in place of the **genuflection** when making a reverence toward the consecrated eucharistic elements. Formerly, bows of the body were distinguished into profound bows and moderate bows. Now, only the profound bow is described, and the priest is directed to bend slightly while pronouncing the words of Christ in the eucharistic prayer. A bow of the head is made as a sign of reverence when the three divine persons are mentioned or when the name of Jesus, Mary, or the saint of the day is mentioned. (GIRM 234)

BREAD (1) – *Bread*, along with wine, constitute the **matter** of the sacrament of the eucharist. These two basic elements find their origin in the ritual for the **Passover** meal and were prayed over by Jesus at the **Last Supper**. The bread must be made solely from wheat flour and water, and, for the Roman Rite, must be unleavened. It should appear as food, and, ideally, one large loaf should be used, which is broken into many pieces, and from these all present (both ministers and others in the assembly) partake at communion. The wafer breads commonly used at Mass are usually called **hosts**. (GIRM 283)

BREAKING OF THE BREAD (1) – The title given to the ritual action of dividing the common loaf of eucharistic bread into many particles to be distributed to the assembly at communion. In the Roman Mass, it takes place after the recitation of the Lord's Prayer and the sign of peace, and right before the invitation to participate in communion. While the action takes place, the hymn *Agnus Dei* ("Lamb of God") is sung. The ritual action is based on the biblical references to the action of Jesus at the Last Supper (cf. Mt 26:26, Lk 24:30,35), and in the Acts of the Apostles (2:42) the *breaking of the bread* seems to be a title given to the entire eucharistic liturgy. (GIRM 56c)

BREVIARY (3) – The name commonly given to the book containing the **liturgy of the hours** (sometimes also called the **divine office**), and sometimes to the prayer itself. The word is derived from the Latin word for "abridgement" or "summary," since the format used by most priests was an abridgement of the monastic format that often needed several books for a single office.

BUGIA (3) – A special candlestick and candle, formerly held near the altar Missal when a bishop celebrated Mass.

BURSE (3) – A flat pocket-like container, about eight inches square, covered with the same cloth as the priest's chasuble, into which the **corporal** could be placed. This was a standard liturgical article required by the Tridentine Missal, but it is no longer mentioned in the present Missal. *Burse* may also refer to the smaller, black, purse-like container, frequently attached to a string, into which a **pyx** for bringing communion to the sick can be placed.

BYZANTINE CHRISTIANITY (3) – The practice of Christianity by those Orthodox and Catholic Christians who use the **Byzantine Rite**. It is frequently associated with long and elaborate ceremonies and ornate and icon-filled churches. Theological writings of Byzantine Christian authors exhibit more reflection on the Holy Spirit, and a greater passivity to God's activity in their lives.

BYZANTINE RITE (3) – The ritual system which developed from the city of Byzantium, renamed Constantinople, and now called Istanbul in what is presently Turkey. It is the second largest **rite** used in the Catholic Church, after the **Roman Rite**, and is used by Orthodox Christians as well. Byzantine Rite churches are distinguished by an **iconastasis**, and the liturgy is celebrated with much singing, incense and symbolism.

CALENDAR (1) – A liturgical *calendar* is a listing of dates of the year with the corresponding feasts celebrated on those dates. Nations, regions, dioceses, and religious institutes may have their own special calendars. Calendars form the basic skeleton for which the yearly sanctification of **time** may take place. (GIRM 314; Gen. Norms for the Liturgical Year and the Calendar 49)

CAMPBELL, JOSEPH (b. 1904) (3) – Author of several books on myths and religions. He is an important figure in the modern understanding of religious experience.

CANDLE (1) – A lamp that has a living flame. (GIRM 79, 269) Former regulations required that the composition of Mass candles and of the **Easter candle** had to be over half beeswax. However, now only the **sanctuary lamp** must be of wax or oil (cf. Introduction to *Holy Communion and Worship of the Eucharist outside Mass* 11).

CANDLE, PASCHAL – See Easter Candle.

CANDLEMAS (3) – An alternate name for the feast of the Purification of Mary, now officially called the *Presentation of the Lord*, celebrated on February 2. The name is derived from the blessing of candles and procession which may be celebrated as part of the introductory rites.

CANON (2) – Older name for the **eucharistic prayer**, especially the section after the **Sanctus**. It is still used in the sub-title of Eucharistic Prayer I of the 1970 Roman Missal, i.e., the *Roman Canon*. (GIRM 322a)

CANONICAL HOURS (2) – The liturgies of prayer and praise that form the **liturgy of the hours** and are celebrated at certain prescribed times of the day. The hours now used are **morning prayer** (formerly called *lauds*), mid-morning prayer (*terce*), mid-day prayer (*sext*), mid-afternoon prayer (*none*), **evening prayer** (*vespers*), **night prayer** (*compline*), and the office of readings (derived from the former office of *matins*). The former hour of *prime* has been suppressed, and those who regularly pray the liturgy of the hours usually celebrate only one of the three hours between morning prayer and evening prayer.

CANOPY (3) – Normally, *canopy* refers to a portable cloth canopy supported by four poles under which a priest may carry the **blessed sacrament** in procession. It also refers to the **baldachino** of the altar, and to a small canopy that used to be required over a bishop's **throne**.

CANTICLE (2) – A hymn, particularly one taken from sacred Scripture, though *not* from the **psalms**. During **morning prayer**, the second selection during the psalmody is a *canticle* taken from the Old Testament, and during **evening prayer**, the third selection during the psalmody is a *canticle* taken from the New Testament.

CANTOR (1) – A person who leads the singing of the assembly at a liturgy, and who may even sing a solo, such as the psalm. (GIRM 67, 78)

CASEL, ODO (1886–1948) (3) – Monk of the Benedictine monastery of **Maria Laach**. He developed the "mystery-theology" as an attempt to explain how the divine is present in Christian worship, the first of modern attempts to develop contemporary theologies about the liturgy. He suffered a stroke as he began to intone the **Exsúltet** at the Easter Vigil in 1948 and died a few hours later.

CASSOCK (2) – The (usually) black, floor-length robe frequently worn by all clerics until the late 1960's. Now cassocks are usually worn by priests only in some European countries and by bishops. However, it is common for **servers** to wear a black or red cassock and a **surplice** while assisting during Mass.

CATECHUMEN (2) – Someone participating in the **R.C.I.A.** and thus preparing to become a Christian and to receive **baptism**. Catechumens may be present during certain Masses for the **liturgy of the word**, but are formally dismissed after the homily to attend a catechetical session based on the Scriptures just read. If they are considered ready to receive baptism, they are "called" during a rite held on the first Sunday of Lent, and then are designated **elect**.

CATECHUMENATE (2) – An extended period of Christian formation prior to adult baptism. It is the second of four stages of the **R.C.I.A.**, the others being the stage of evangelization, **enlightenment**, and **mystagogy**. However, the term is sometimes loosely used to refer to the entire R.C.I.A. process.

CATHEDRA (3) – The bishop's chair (**throne**) in a **cathedral**, a sign of the bishop's leadership over his flock. It is used by the bishop as the **presidential chair** when he is presider at any liturgical service.

CATHEDRAL (2) – The head church in a diocese, at which the **bishop** should preside over major liturgies. In the cathedral, the bishop's **cathedra** has a place of honor.

CELEBRANT (1) – The term that usually refers to the presiding minister at a worship service. However, many contemporary writers emphasize that the **assembly** as a whole is really the *celebrant* at any worship service, under the leadership of one individual designated as the **presider**. Hence, the term "presider" is used more and more in preference to *celebrant*.

CELEBRATE (1) – The term designating the execution of a worship service, e.g., "Mass is *celebrated*." As with the secular meaning of the word, the term presumes a gathering of people, a variety of emotions, and special actions such as processions and song. (GIRM 1)

CENSER (2) – A vessel in which **incense** resins may be burned to produce sweet-smelling smoke. Originally, censers were open bowls left in stationary positions, or shovel-like containers with handles. Now they are usually covered vessels suspended by one or more chains and, in the Roman Rite, held mid-way along the chains while swung toward the object being reverenced. In the Eastern Rites, the censer is usually swung at the full-length of the chains. It is also called a **thurible**. (GIRM 236)

CEREMONIAL OF BISHOPS (3) – An official book of directions and **rubrics** for bishops to aid them in celebrating the Mass, the sacraments, and other liturgies. The rubrics of the *Ceremonial* are much more detailed than those in the **Missal**, and thus frequently the Ceremonial is an aid to understanding the (possibly confusing) rubrics in the Missal.

CHAIR, PRESIDENTIAL (1) – The special chair reserved for use by the presiding priest at a liturgy. The chair is a symbol of the presence of the teaching Christ, who himself sat before teaching (cf. Sermon on the Mount, Mt 5:1). Thus it is different from the **sedilia** of the Tridentine Mass, a place solely for the ministers to *rest* when not required to be elsewhere. In the present Roman Mass, the chair is one of three focal points of the **sanctuary** (along with the **ambo** and the **altar**) and is a significant and liturgically symbolic place, being the proper location for the presiding priest to be at certain points of the liturgy. During Mass, the presiding priest should be at the chair during the introductory rites (after the entrance procession), the liturgy of the word (unless he needs to proclaim the gospel when there is no deacon), and the concluding rite. The presiding priest or bishop may even give the homily seated at the chair. (GIRM 271; LM 26)

CHALICE (1) – The older name for the **cup** used to hold the **wine** for the eucharist.

CHALICE VEIL (2) – A square veil that is draped over the chalice at the **credence table** during the liturgy of the word. Formerly, the veil matched the cloth and color of the priest's **chasuble**, but now it may always be white. (GIRM 80c)

CHANCEL (3) – The area close to the altar for the clergy. In some churches, this may include the **choir** area in addition to the **sanctuary**, and may be partitioned from the **nave** (i.e., the area for the laity) by a **rood screen**.

CHAPEL, RESERVATION (2) – The area in a church, ideally separated from the main section, in which the **tabernacle** to reserve the eucharistic bread is located. (GIRM 276; EACW 28–29)

CHASUBLE (2) – The outer **vestment** of presbyters and bishops while celebrating the eucharist. It resembles a sleeve-less poncho and follows the sequence of **liturgical colors**. (GIRM 299)

CHASUBLE, FOLDED – See Folded Chasuble.

CHOIR (1) – A special group of singers, who assist the assembly with singing (but do not substitute for it). (GIRM 274) *Choir* may also designate a section of the church building, or a separate chapel, where seats (*"choir" stalls*) are arranged along the walls so that one half of the assembly faces the other half, especially where the assembly prays the **liturgy of the hours** (*"in choir"*).

CHRISM (2) – An oil specially blessed by the bishop at the **chrism Mass** that is used at the baptism of infants, at confirmation, at the ordination of priests and bishops, and at the dedication of a church and altar. Ideally, *chrism* is a perfume to which a little oil is added to dilute it, though in practice it is an oil to which a little perfume has been added to make it smell pleasant. It is stored in vials (**stocks**) labeled *S.C.* (for *Sacred Chrism*).

CHRISM MASS (2) – The Mass celebrated on **Holy Thursday** morning (or close to it) at which the bishop of the diocese blesses the **chrism**, the **oil of the sick**, and the **oil of catechumens**. It has also become a special Mass at which the ministerial priestly commitment is renewed. In the Tridentine Missal, the *chrism Mass* was unusual in that communion of the faithful was forbidden. (GIRM, 53)

CHRISMATION (3) – The name given to the sacrament of **confirmation** by the Eastern Orthodox Church.

CHRIST THE KING, SOLEMNITY OF (2) – The solemnity now celebrated in late November on the last Sunday of Ordinary Time (which also is the Sunday before the First Sunday of Advent). This observance was introduced in 1925 by Pope Pius XI and at that time assigned to the last Sunday in October.

CHRISTMAS (1) – The solemnity of the birth of Christ, observed on December 25. It is preceded by a period of preparation, called the **Advent** season, and the postfestal Christmas **season** continues until the feast of the Baptism of the Lord in early January.

CHRISTOLOGY (3) – The theological discipline that deals with reflection on Jesus Christ, and on his person as being both divine and human. Christologies can be labeled in various ways, e.g., as "descending" (the Word becoming flesh), or "ascending" (Jesus becoming glorified), or by other titles. Worship reflects an implicit *christology*, and the *christology* commonly accepted by a community assembled for worship may consciously or unconsciously shape the worship taking place.

CHURCH (1) – The community of Christians, especially gathered for worship. The building for worship was originally called the "house of the church," but now *church* often refers to the building itself. The word *church* is also used for those involved in the administration of the community of Christians, particularly the **hierarchy**. (GIRM 253; EACW 27, 28)

CHURCHES, CONSECRATION OF – See **Consecration of Churches**.

CHURCHING (3) – A blessing of mothers celebrated after childbirth. It seems to have its origin in the rite of purification of mothers required by Leviticus 12:1–8. In the revised rite for the baptism of children, a special blessing is provided for the mother that takes the place of the separate rite in the old **Roman Ritual**. However, the revised **Book of Blessings** provides for the blessing of a mother who was unable to be present for the baptism of her child.

CIBORIUM (2) – (Plural: *ciboria*) The goblet-like vessels used for the eucharistic bread. Contemporary ciboria are more commonly made in the form of plates or bowls. Both styles frequently are made with a covering lid, and special veils were formerly required when ciboria containing the consecrated bread were stored in **tabernacles**. The **canopy** or **baldachino** over an altar is sometimes called a *ciborium*. (GIRM 80c, 292)

CINCTURE (2) – The rope belt used to fasten an **alb** at the waist. Its use is now optional. (GIRM 298)

CLERICALISM (2) – The attitude of mind in which clergy are seen to be somehow better than laity. This is occasionally evident when clerics usurp liturgical roles properly held by a lay person (cf. GIRM 66).

CLOSING PRAYER (2) – A misnomer, usually referring to the **prayer after communion**.

COLLECT (2) – The opening prayer of the liturgy, the first **presidential prayer** offered by the presiding priest. It sums up and *collects* all the thoughts and prayers of the assembly, and concludes the **introductory rites**. After the *collect* everyone is seated and the liturgy of the word begins. In structure and function, it is not primarily a preparation prayer for the liturgy of the word, since, by tradition, the same prayer used as the collect of the Mass is also used as the concluding prayer for **morning prayer** and **evening prayer**. In the Good Friday service, the collect is the only text of the introductory rites. (GIRM 10, 32)

COLLECTION (1) – The action of collecting money for the church and the poor that usually takes place at Mass after the **general intercessions** and before the procession and preparation of the gifts. This is commonly done by **ushers**. (GIRM 49, 101)

COLORS, LITURGICAL (2) – The official colors of the outer **vestments** worn by the presiding priest. Certain seasons and feasts normally require specific colors. By tradition in the Roman Rite, the colors are white, green, red, violet, black and rose, and the determination of which color is used when is found in the Missal. More precious vestments (usually with gold or silver threads) may be used on solemn occasions. Many Eastern Rites have no set colors, except that dark reds are used at funerals and during Lent. Some liturgists have recently suggested that a deep bluish-purple (sign of night and waiting) be used during **Advent** to distinguish it from a reddish-purple (sign of pain and suffering) during **Lent**. (GIRM 307–310)

COMMEMORATION (2) – This is the title of a classification sometimes given to a **memorial** during special privileged seasons of the church year, such as during Lent. In privileged seasons, a memorial is observed at Mass only by use of the proper **collect**; all other texts come from the seasonal texts. (Gen. Instruction of the Liturgy of the Hours 238–239; cf. GIRM 316)

COMMENTATOR (2) – The minister who provides commentaries or explanations to the assembly of the sacred texts or actions. (GIRM 68a)

COMMINGLING (2) – The rite of dropping a small particle of the consecrated bread into the cup. It occurs in the Mass after the **breaking of the bread** and seems to have its origin in the rite of dropping a piece of bread (called the **fermentum**) consecrated by the pope and brought to the celebrations in the outlying areas of Rome. (GIRM 56d)

COMMISSIONING (2) – A rite of authorizing and blessing individuals for some ministry. This title is usually given to the rite of designating individuals as **special** or **extraordinary ministers** of the eucharist.

COMMON PRAYER, BOOK OF (3) – The title of the main service book of the Church of England and other member churches of the Anglican Communion. Some other Protestant churches also use this title. It includes texts for the celebration of the eucharist, various sacraments, other services (e.g. funerals), and the divine office.

COMMUNAL PENANCE SERVICE (2) – A service of penitential readings, hymns and prayers, frequently (but not always) associated with the reception of the sacrament of **penance**. Oftentimes, *communal penance services* include (or are followed by) the opportunity for the individual celebration of the sacrament of penance with the individual reception of **absolution**, although in special circumstances general absolution may be imparted in the communal service itself.

COMMUNION (1) – The action of receiving the consecrated elements of bread and wine. *Communion* sometimes is used of the elements themselves. (GIRM 56)

COMMUNION RAIL (2) – The railing commonly found at the edge of the sanctuary in older churches, at which communicants used to kneel while receiving communion.

COMMUNION SERVICE (2) – The name given to a service of the word of God at which the eucharistic bread, consecrated at a previous Mass, is distributed to the assembly. Such services may be held in those places lacking enough priests to celebrate Mass, and are led by deacons or authorized lay leaders of prayer. The most common form of *communion service* follows the pattern of the Mass, except that the preparation of the gifts and the eucharistic prayer are omitted, and a hymn of praise may be sung instead. Some non-Catholic churches regularly call their **eucharist** a *communion service*.

COMMUNION UNDER BOTH KINDS (2) – The rite of distributing both the consecrated bread and also the consecrated wine to the assembly at Mass. Distributing the consecrated wine to the assembly had fallen into disuse for several centuries, but has been once again authorized by the Second Vatican Council. Four methods are allowed in the present Missal: drinking from the cup, **intinction**, using a **straw**, or using a **spoon**. (GIRM 240–252)

COMMUNITY MASS (2) – The major daily Mass celebrated by members of a religious community, usually in the chapel of the religious community. The *community Mass* is the common title given to the Mass celebrated by those religious who are *not* bound to celebrate the **liturgy of the hours** in choir. Those who celebrate the liturgy of the hours in choir usually refer to their major Mass as the **conventual Mass**. (GIRM 76, 242.14)

COMPLINE (3) – The older name for **night prayer**, one of the **canonical hours**.

CONCELEBRANT (2) – Someone who **celebrates** a liturgical service along *with* others. In the broadest sense, every member of the assembly is a concelebrant of the sacred action. However, the word usually refers to priests who join the presiding priest according to prescribed rubrical norms. Although *concelebrant* normally is associated with the eucharist (a **concelebration**), it can also refer to other liturgical services. At the ordination of a bishop, at least three bishops must concelebrate the ordination rite, imposing hands and reciting the consecratory prayer. In the Byzantine Rite, the anointing of the sick is ideally concelebrated by seven priests, each of whom anoints the sick person on a different part of the body. (GIRM 161–208)

CONCELEBRATION (2) – Normally, *concelebration* refers to that form of Mass in which several priests participate according to prescribed norms, and together vocalize part of the eucharistic prayer. Because they all say the words of Christ, considered to be the **form** of the sacrament, they are considered to be ministers of the sacrament along with the presiding priest. Except for Masses of ordination, concelebration was forbidden in the Roman Rite before the Second Vatican Council, though it was common in almost all Eastern Rites. To the extent that concelebration eliminates the older custom of several priests saying Mass independently (privately), frequently at the same time at different altars in the same church, it brings out the unity of priesthood and the people of God at the eucharist. To the extent that the present liturgical form separates the ordained from the non-ordained, it has become more and more of a topic for discussion and further theological reflection. (GIRM 153–160)

CONCLUDING RITE (2) – The last section of the Mass, following the **liturgy of the eucharist**. It consists of brief announcements, a greeting, a blessing, and the dismissal of the assembly. After the dismissal, the ministers return to the sacristy. If some special rite follows the Mass, such as the **final commendation** at a funeral, the entire *concluding rite* is omitted.

CONFESSION (1) – The common name for the sacrament of **penance**, although the actual *confession* of sins is only one part of the total rite. Prior to Vatican II, many Catholics "went to confession" before each reception of communion.

CONFESSIONAL (2) – The room or structure where the sacrament of **penance** is celebrated. *Confessional* frequently refers to the traditional structure, in which a priest sits in a center chair and penitents kneel on either side, speaking through opaque grates. The more contemporary arrangement, in which a penitent is able to either remain anonymous or face the priest, is usually referred to as a **reconciliation room**.

CONFIRMATION (1) – The sacrament that continues the initiation process begun in the sacrament of **baptism** and prepares an individual for the culmination of initiation through participation in the eucharist. Unfortunately, except for those baptized as adults, confirmation is usually received by many people *after* they have been admitted to communion. In the case of those baptized as infants, *confirmation* is conferred by a **bishop** who anoints the individuals with **chrism**, after first imposing hands over all to be confirmed.

CONFÍTEOR (2) – The common name for the confession proclamation used during one of the **penitential rites** of Mass. The name is derived from the first word of the Latin version which begins: *Confíteor Deo omnipoténti* ("I confess to almighty God"). In the Tridentine Mass, the *Confíteor* was also recited before the distribution of communion to the assembly. The present text is an abbreviation of the version in the Tridentine Missal.

CONGREGATION (1) – The community of Christians gathered for worship, also called the **assembly**. Sometimes the term is used to designate the "people in the pews" to distinguish them from the choir and the sanctuary ministers. (GIRM 82, 273)

CONGREGATION FOR DIVINE WORSHIP (3) – The usual title for the *Congregation for Divine Worship and the Discipline of the Sacraments*, one of the congregations of the Roman Curia. This congregation and others in the Roman Curia were last reorganized in June, 1988, and the present structure combines what were two separate congregations. This congregation has been given authority over things pertaining to the liturgy and sacraments in the Roman Rite. It can issue documents, revise liturgical rites, and approve vernacular translations.

CONOPAEUM (3) – Older Latin name for the **tabernacle veil**.

CONSECRATION (1) – A making holy and setting apart through prayer. The term now is used only for the sacrament of the eucharist, and for the setting apart of women committed to a life of virginity. The **institution narrative** section of the eucharistic prayer is considered to be essential to the *consecration* of the elements of bread and wine. (GIRM 55d)

CONSECRATION OF BISHOPS (3) – Older name for the **ordination** of bishops. The term is no longer used in the liturgical texts for the ordination rite, although it is still used in canon 379 of the 1983 Code of Canon Law.

CONSECRATION OF CHURCHES (3) – Older name for the **dedication of churches**.

CONSECRATION, SUPPLEMENTAL (2) – The rite practiced by many local churches in the Anglican Communion of consecrating additional bread or wine if the elements previously consecrated do not suffice for the number of communicants. The only parallel practice allowed in the Catholic tradition is the supplemental consecration of wine if it were discovered that the chalice did not actually contain wine during the eucharistic prayer. (cf. GIRM 286)

CONSENT (3) – The traditional term found in theological and canonical writings for the marriage vows. The term goes back to ancient Rome, and (as used in the liturgical texts and canon law) implies the internal covenant of love and life and the external expression of that covenant through the words of the vows. (cf. canons 1057, 1096, and 1108)

CONSILIUM (3) – The common title for the *Consilium ad exsequendam Constitutionem de sacra Liturgia*, a special commission which was established in 1964 and absorbed into the Congregation for Divine Worship in 1970. It consisted of two main groups: forty (full) members (mostly cardinals and bishops) who had deliberative vote, and a much larger group of *consultors*, who were most often experts in liturgy or liturgical history. It was this body that revised the order of Mass and the rites of the various sacraments. Among its consultors were **Bernard Botte, O.S.B., Godfrey Diekmann, O.S.B., Josef Jungmann, S.J.,** and **Frederick McManus**.

CONSTITUTION ON THE SACRED LITURGY (2) – The first decree of the Second Vatican Council, also known by its Latin title, **Sacrosanctum Concilium**. It was promulgated on December 4, 1963, and, in particular, allowed the celebration of liturgical rites in the vernacular, called for the active participation of the assembly present, and ordered the revision of all liturgical rites.

CONSUBSTANTIATION (3) – A theological term used by Lutherans to explain Christ's presence in the eucharistic bread and wine after the proclamation of the eucharistic prayer. It asserts that Christ's body and blood are present *with* (*con-*) the bread and wine.

CONVENTUAL MASS (2) – The major daily Mass celebrated by members of a religious community, usually in the chapel of the religious community. The *conventual Mass* is the common title given to the Mass celebrated by those religious who *are* bound to celebrate the **liturgy of the hours** in choir. Those who do not celebrate the liturgy of the hours in choir usually refer to their major Mass as the **community Mass**. (GIRM 76, 242.14)

COPE (2) – A long cape-like vestment, usually of the same color and material as a chasuble. It may be worn in processions joined to a Mass, or at more solemn liturgical celebrations that occur apart from Mass. (GIRM 303)

CORPORAL (2) – The cloth on which the vessels containing bread and wine are placed on the altar. It is traditionally square, and when not in use, folded into thirds in both directions. It is placed on top of the altar cloth during the preparation of the altar and gifts, and in a sense resembles a place mat at a formal dinner. (GIRM 49, 80c, 100)

CORPUS CHRISTI (2) – The former name of the solemnity of the **Body and Blood of Christ**.

COVENANT SERVICE (3) – A Methodist rite celebrated usually on a Sunday near the beginning of the calendar year. It is a renewal service intended to focus on the whole of Christian life. It contains a covenant prayer: "I am no longer my own, but yours . . . "

CRANMER, THOMAS (1489–1556) (3) – Archbishop of Canterbury at the time of King Henry VIII and the establishment of the independent Church of England. He was responsible for the change of the Latin rites into English and for the compilation of the first two Anglican **Books of Common Prayer** of 1549 and 1552.

CREDENCE TABLE (2) – The common name given to the side table on which the vessels and articles needed for the celebration are placed when not in use. (cf. GIRM 80c)

CREED (1) – Alternate name for the **profession of faith**.

CROSIER (2) – The common name for what is technically called the *pastoral staff* of a bishop. In western churches, it is normally shaped like a shepherd's crook. In some eastern churches, the top of the staff has two snakes intertwined and facing each other, symbolic of the staffs of Moses and Aaron which turned into snakes (Ex 4:2–3, 7:9). In the Roman Rite, the bishop holds the staff while walking in the entrance procession and in the recessional, while the gospel is proclaimed, and during solemn blessings. He may also hold it while giving the homily and at other times determined by the rubrics or by custom. From the 11th century until the pontificate of Pope Paul VI, the pope did not use a *crosier*, but Paul VI started to use a staff surmounted by a crucifix as a crosier which his successors have also used.

CROSS (1) – Any representation of the cross on which Christ died. Each church should have a cross visible to the assembly. However, this cross does not have to be seen by the presiding priest at Mass, nor need it have the image of Christ on it. (GIRM 236, 270)

CROSS, PECTORAL (2) – By custom, bishops in the Roman Rite wear a cross at chest height (*pectoral*), suspended from a chain around their necks. Many eastern bishops wear a pectoral icon rather than a cross, and some Russian priests wear a pectoral cross also. Bishops by custom wear the cross under the chasuble at Mass, although in recent years, some bishops are wearing the cross over the chasuble.

CROSS, PROCESSIONAL (2) – A cross, mounted on a pole, that may be carried in processions. The cross-bearer, between two candle-bearers and following the thurifer (if incense is used), customarily leads processions, at least on more solemn occasions. The processional cross carried before an archbishop may have an additional cross bar. (GIRM 82b, 84)

CROSS, SIGN OF THE (1) – The gesture made by touching the tips of the fingers of the right hand to the forehead, mid-chest, left shoulder, and right shoulder (or, in the

Byzantine Rite, the right shoulder before the left shoulder). It is usually accompanied by a trinitarian formula taken from the baptismal command at the end of Matthew's gospel, "In the name of the Father, and of the Son, and of the Holy Spirit." (GIRM 28)

CRUCIFIX (2) – A **cross** that has an image of Christ ("the crucified") on it.

CRUET (2) – A (small) pitcher-like vessel containing the wine or water for the eucharist. (GIRM 80c, 103)

CUFFS (3) – Liturgical vestments for a priest in the Byzantine Rite. They serve to gather together the large ends of the sleeves of the Byzantine style *stichar* (**alb**), and are usually made of the same material as the outer vestment, the **phelon (chasuble)**.

CULT (3) – A system of worship, with particular reference to external ceremonies. The word can refer both to rites comprising divine worship, and also to the devotions by which external honor is given to saints. It also is used to indicate certain types of religious groups.

CULTURAL ADAPTATION (3) – Changes in the liturgical rites due to pastoral responses to the local culture. Major *cultural adaptation* takes the forms of **acculturation** and **inculturation**. (cf. GIRM 6, 232)

CUP (2) – The goblet or **chalice** used to hold the wine for the eucharist. Ideally, only one *cup* should be used on the altar until the **breaking of the bread**. At that point, other cups used for distributing communion under both kinds may be brought to the altar and the consecrated wine poured into them. (GIRM 289, 291)

CYRIL OF ALEXANDRIA (d. 444) (3) – Bishop of Alexandria, elected in 412. He was a theologian at the Council of Ephesus, who opposed the Nestorians and defended the title of Mary as *Theotokos*, a title used in the Byzantine liturgy to this day. He is considered to be a doctor of the Western Church.

CYRIL OF JERUSALEM (d. 387) (3) – Bishop of Jerusalem from around 349 until his death, and author of the *Mystagogical Catecheses*, a series of lectures to the newly-baptized. In these lectures we find a description of the various sacramental and eucharistic rites, particularly a description of how to receive communion in the hand: "make your left hand a throne for the right, since it is to receive a king" (Lect 5:21). He is quoted as supporting the theology that says that it is the **epiclesis** or invocation of the Holy Spirit that effects the change of bread and wine into the body of blood of Christ: "the bread of the eucharist, after the invocation of the Holy Spirit, is mere bread no longer, but the body of Christ" (Lect 3:3), "for whatsoever the Holy Spirit has touched is sanctified and changed" (Lect 5:7). He insisted that worship is indivisible. He had great influence in the rites of Holy Week, and the elaborate and extensive rites he celebrated were documented by the pilgrim nun, **Egeria**. (Introduction to GIRM 8)

DALMATIC (2) – The outer vestment proper to a deacon. It is usually made of the same cloth as a **chasuble**, but cut so that the garment has sleeves. The *dalmatic* and the subdeacon's **tunic** were usually distinguished only in that the dalmatic had two decorative cross bars (sometimes called *orphreys*) whereas the tunic had only one. A bishop wears a thin dalmatic under his chasuble when celebrating a **stational Mass**. (GIRM 300)

DANCE, LITURGICAL (2) – Dance as incorporated into official worship. Dance has been a traditional part of the Ethiopian and Syriac liturgies during the chanting of psalms. A rhythmic movement of the assembly accompanies the singing of the Gloria during the Zairean Mass. This kind of stylized dance is performed also by the Zairean clergy as they circle around the altar while incensing it. A stylized processional dance is part of the Byzantine wedding ritual when the priest leads the newly-married and crowned couple around the icon stand three times. Interpretive dancing during music, song, or the reading of a text, has been used as an experimental form of liturgical prayer in some communities, although there has been no official approbation of such a practice.

DANIÉLOU, JEAN (1905–1974) (3) – French Jesuit and later Cardinal. He rediscovered patristic exegesis, both of scripture and of liturgy. He was the author of numerous works, in particular, *The Bible and the Liturgy*.

DEACON (1) – The assistant minister whose liturgical duties particularly involve reading the gospel passage and assisting with the cup. The deacon is the first rank of the three-fold ministerial structure of the sacrament of **holy orders**. This rank finds its origins in the selection of "deacons" in Acts 6 and in 1 Timothy 3:8. In some places, a particular ministry of the deacon is to encourage the active participation of the assembly. (GIRM 61, 127–141; Ceremonial of Bishops 26)

DEACONESS (3) – A female minister whose major duties were to assist in the baptism and anointing of women. Although deaconesses were common in some parts of the east, they long since ceased to exist. Ancient texts for the blessing and installation of deaconesses have been found, but it is unclear whether or not they were considered as equivalent to male **deacons**.

DEDICATION OF CHURCHES (2) – The formal, solemn blessing of a church building, usually by a bishop. The walls may be anointed with **chrism** and special crosses may be affixed inside of a church so blessed (the *consecration crosses*). This rite was formerly called a **consecration**. (cf. GIRM 255)

DIDACHE (3) – An early Christian collection of catechetical and liturgical texts, parts of which seem to date to the mid-first century of the Christian era. Many suggest it was edited around the year **75**. The title is the Greek word for *Teaching*. Contained in the *Didache* are the texts for the Lord's Prayer, the rite of baptism, regulations on fasting, and prayers over the bread and cup. It is uncertain whether the prayers over the bread and cup were used at a eucharist in our sense, or at an **agape** meal, or whether any distinction would have been made.

DIEKMANN, GODFREY (b. 1908) (3) – American Benedictine liturgist and author of *Come, Let us Worship* (among other works). He was editor-in-chief of *Worship* journal from 1938 until the early 1980's and is presently editor emeritus. He was one of the few Americans who was a consultor to the post-conciliar commission (**Consilium**) that revised the order of Mass.

DIES IRAE (3) – The **sequence** for Masses of the dead in the Tridentine Missal. The first verse reads, "Day of wrath, O that day, when creation shall dissolve into embers, as David and the Sybil testified." This sequence has been dropped in the revised Missal since its sentiments seem contrary to the sense of hope and resurrection found in the revised rites for the dead. Its former presence is recalled particularly in musical settings of **requiems**, for example, those by Berlioz and Verdi.

DIPTYCHS (3) – A double paneled tablet on which the names of those commemorated at the eucharistic liturgy were listed. The term is also used of the list itself, or of the **intercessions** section of the eucharistic prayer in which the living and dead are commemorated.

DIRECTORY FOR MASSES WITH CHILDREN (3) – A 1973 Roman document that described underlying principles to be used when preparing for Masses with children. It also authorized possible adaptations and omissions in such Masses.

DISMISSAL (2) – The final, formal invitation by the deacon (or priest) to the assembly to go forth from the celebration. It may also refer to the *dismissal* of the **catechumens** after the homily. (GIRM 57b)

DIVINE OFFICE (3) – The older name for the **liturgy of the hours**.

DIVINE OFFICE, CATHEDRAL FORM (3) – The structure of daily liturgical prayer that centered (exclusively) around **morning prayer** and **evening prayer** (at dawn and sunset). These offices of prayer were tied to the times of the day: morning prayer was related to praise for creation and resurrection, and evening prayer was related to petition and intercession for salvation. Both consisted of a limited number of psalms, hymns, scriptural readings and prayers, and were celebrated by the community as a whole, rather than by a small group of clerics or monks.

DIVINE OFFICE, MONASTIC FORM (3) – The structure of daily liturgical prayer that centered on a continuous praying of the psalms and Scripture, and was geared for an immobile, stable community, as found in a monastery. From this form there developed the night office and the various mid-day prayers. The monastic form exerted its influence on the cathedral form, eventually forcing the incorporation of all the monastic **canonical hours** of prayer into the common **liturgy of the hours** as used by communities not centered in a monastery.

DIX, GREGORY (1901–1952) (3) – British Anglican monk and liturgist, and author of *The Shape of the Liturgy* (among other works). It was in this work that the fourfold structure of the liturgy of the eucharist (i.e., TAKE, BLESS, BREAK, SHARE) was first discussed.

DOUGLAS, MARY (b. 1921) (3) – British anthropologist, particularly concerned with human symbols and the link to culture. Her work (and that of Victor Turner) is foundational for **inculturation** of the liturgy.

DOXOLOGY (2) – A hymn or prayer of praise and **worship** of God. The **Gloria** is sometimes called the "Great Doxology," and the prayer "Glory to the Father, and to the Son, . . . " is sometimes called the "Minor Doxology." Endings to certain prayers are also termed *doxologies* if "praise" or "glory" is mentioned, such as the conclusion of the eucharistic prayer ("Through him, . . . all glory and honor is yours, . . . ") and of the Lord's Prayer ("For the kingdom . . . the glory are yours . . . ").

DRAMA, LITURGICAL (2) – Dramatic presentations of scriptural or hagiographical scenarios woven into the liturgy, especially as part of the homily. The annual solemn proclamations of the passion on **Passion [Palm] Sunday** and **Good Friday** are a form of *liturgical drama* in that various readers take various dramatic "roles" throughout the proclamations while a narrator reads the rest of the text. Solemn baptism by immersion also may be considered to be a liturgical drama in that it is a dramatic reenactment of Christ's own baptism. However, some liturgists make a distinction between liturgical *remembrance* and dramatic **reenactment**, and insist that liturgy must fundamentally be a *remembrance*. Remembrance or **anamnesis** is a here-and-now action, whereas reenactment and, to a great extent, *drama* tends to remain on the level of a passive historical mirroring of a past event.

DULIA (2) – Honor given to holy men and women now in God's presence in heaven. Prayers and devotions to saints are *dulia* rather than the formal **latria** or worship given to God or Christ.

The Dictionary

EASTER (1) – The day that commemorates the resurrection of Jesus, celebrated on the first Sunday after the first full moon after the vernal equinox (about March 21). Its celebration continues for 50 days and concludes with Pentecost Sunday. (GIRM 308a)

EASTER CANDLE (2) – The special candle blessed, inscribed, lighted, and carried in procession at the beginning of the **Easter Vigil**. It is lit during Masses and other services throughout the fifty days of the Easter season. After Pentecost, it is kept in the **baptistery** and lit during the celebration of baptism. It may also be used at funerals, placed at the head of the coffin.

EASTER VIGIL (1) – The "mother of all vigils" (**Augustine**, *Sermo* 219), celebrated on the evening and during the night before Easter Sunday. This vigil service includes the ancient practice of blessing new fire and lighting a special **Easter candle** at the beginning of the service, followed by the procession and proclamation of Christ's resurrection through the solemn **Exsúltet**. Then follows an elongated liturgy of the word, and a liturgy of baptism, during which the **catechumens** are baptized and all present renew their own baptismal commitment. The service concludes with the liturgy of the eucharist during which the newly-baptized receive communion for the first time. For several centuries, this Vigil was actually celebrated on the *morning* of Holy Saturday, but in 1951, Pope Pius XII allowed the experimental restoration of the Vigil to the evening. In 1955, Pope Pius XII issued a decree revising many of the liturgies of Holy Week and officially restored the Easter Vigil to its original place as an evening night-watch of the Lord's resurrection. The morning celebration of the Vigil resulted in the former practice of considering Lent (and its penances of fasting and abstinence) to be concluded at noon on Holy Saturday.

ECCLESIOLOGY (3) – A theology of the Church. As with other theological areas (e.g. **christology**), an implicit *ecclesiology* is evident in any liturgy, and certain liturgical forms help perpetuate certain ecclesiological models.

ECONOMY (3) – A term derived from the Greek word for *household management*, and used for God's *plan of salvation*, especially as referred to by Paul in Ephesians 3:9. The divine *economy* is proclaimed and celebrated in the liturgy.

EGERIA (c. 350-c. 400) (3) – A visitor to Jerusalem between 381 and 384, while **Cyril of Jerusalem** was bishop. Her writings suggest she was a Spanish nun. She left a fairly detailed account of the liturgy as celebrated in Jerusalem in that era, particularly of the rites of Holy Week. The name is sometimes spelled *Etheria*.

ELECT (2) – Those **catechumens** preparing for baptism who have been "chosen" through the rite of election as ready to receive baptism. The *elect* are usually designated as such on the First Sunday of Lent. During Lent, the **scrutinies** are celebrated with them, normally at Mass on the Third, Fourth and Fifth Sundays of Lent.

ELEMENTS (2) – A common title usually referring to both the bread and wine of the eucharist, e.g. *the sacred elements*. (GIRM 7)

ELEVATION (2) – The lifting up of the bread (on the plate) and the cup during the **eucharistic prayer**. In the Tridentine Missal, the showing of the bread and cup after the words of consecration was called the "major" *elevation*, and the lifting of both the bread and cup at the final doxology of the eucharistic prayer was called the "minor" *elevation*. These titles corresponded to the relative height of elevating the elements. In the revised Missal, the title is no longer used, but there still are two prescribed liftings of the elements during the eucharistic prayer. The first lifting of the elements individually after the words of consecration is done so that the assembly might see the bread and cup. This *elevation* need not be very high, since now the presiding priest is normally facing the rest of the assembly. The second lifting of the elements together during the final doxology by the presiding priest and deacon is now construed as the "major" *elevation*, and should be seen as a gesture of "offering," presenting the consecrated elements in the sight of God and the gathered assembly.

ELIADE, MIRCEA (b. 1907) (3) – Historian of religions and author of *The Sacred and the Profane: The Nature of Religion*. He has been very influential in the modern reflection on the nature of religious ritual activity.

ELLARD, GERALD (1894–1963) (3) – American Jesuit liturgist and author of *The Mass of the Future*, and *The Mass in Transition* (among other works).

EMBER DAYS (3) – Special days of prayer and fasting that were omitted in the revision of the **calendar** in 1969. The *ember days* were the Wednesday, Friday, and Saturday of four weeks occurring during the four natural seasons of the year. The designated weeks were the third week of Advent, the first week of Lent, the week after Pentecost, and the week after September 14 (the feast of the Exaltation of the Cross). The national conference of bishops may designate certain days for prayer as a contemporary adaptation of the ember days. (cf. GIRM 331)

EMBOLISM (2) – Any expansion of a phrase. It normally refers to the expansion of the last phrase of the Lord's Prayer, "but deliver us from evil," which is developed into a solemn conclusion to the Lord's Prayer ("Deliver us, Lord, from every evil . . . ") recited by the presiding priest before the final doxology ("For the kingdom, . . . "). (GIRM 56a, 111)

ENERGY (3) – A term used by Eastern Patristic saints, such as **Basil of Caesarea**, to describe that which we can know of God. "God's *energies* come down to us, but His essence remains unapproachable" (*Letter* 234:1). Ultimately, it is cooperation with and openness to divine energies that are celebrated and sought in liturgy.

ENLIGHTENMENT, PERIOD OF (3) – The final period of the **catechumenate** (also called the period of *purification*), between the rite of "election" (on the First Sunday of Lent) and the rites of initiation (at the **Easter Vigil**). Those who are admitted to this stage of the **R.C.I.A.** are called the **elect**.

ENVIRONMENT AND ART IN CATHOLIC WORSHIP (3) – A 1978 document from the U.S. Bishops' Committee on the Liturgy expanding and commenting on Chapter 5 of the GIRM (253–280). It speaks particularly about quality, appropriateness, and authenticity in all things used in the liturgy.

EPICLESIS (2) – A Greek word, derived from the verb *call upon* or *invoke*. In general, *epiclesis* refers to any petition or request, but commonly it is used to refer to the section of the **eucharistic prayer** that requests the Holy Spirit to come upon the elements and the community, so that the community may receive the elements as the body and blood of Christ. An *epiclesis* is termed *consecratory* if the main petition is for a change in the elements, and it is called *communion* if the main petition is for unity in the assembly who partakes of the consecrated elements. In the Roman Missal, two *epicleses* can be discerned in the various eucharistic prayers, one consecratory (before the **institution narrative**) and the other a communion *epiclesis* (after the **anamnesis**). Various authors have examined the relationship between *anamnesis* and *epiclesis* (remembering—invoking) and see it as forming a fundamental structure for all Christian prayer and sacramental activity. (GIRM 55c)

EPIPHANY (2) – The **solemnity** celebrated on January 6 (or the following Sunday) commemorating the visit of the Magi to the newborn Christ child, and thus, the first manifestation or appearing of Jesus to the non-Jewish world. The word is derived from the Greek word for *shining* or *appearing*, and is found in Scripture in Luke 1:79 ("the Dayspring . . . shall *shine* . . . ") or 1 Timothy 6:14 (" . . . the *appearing* of our Lord Jesus Christ"), among other places. The period between Epiphany and the pre-Lenten Sundays was called the "Epiphany season" in the Tridentine Missal and Sundays designated as "Sundays after Epiphany," but now the period is called **Ordinary Time**.

EPISTLE (3) – Technically, an old word for *letter*, and used to refer to the New Testament letters (of Paul, John, etc.). In the Tridentine Missal, except for **ember days** and the **Easter Vigil**, Masses only had two readings from Scripture: one from the gospel preceded by one from the New Testament *epistles* or some other book of the Bible. Even when the first reading was not from an *epistle*, it was still referred to by that title.

EPISTLE SIDE (3) – The right side of the altar and sanctuary, as viewed from the assembly. It was the side at which a **subdeacon** sang the **epistle** during a solemn Mass celebrated according to the Tridentine Missal.

EPITRACHELION (3) – The name for the **stole** as worn by priests of the **Byzantine Rite**. Whereas the two ends of stoles of the Roman Rite are not attached when hanging on a priest, the *epitrachelion* is so made that the two ends are attached along a common edge.

EUCHARIST (1) – A word, derived from Greek, that means *thanksgiving*. The entire action of celebrating the Lord's Supper or Mass is commonly called the *eucharist*, as are the consecrated elements of bread and wine and the word was used as early as in the **Didache** (ch. 9) and by **Justin**. This name is derived from the central prayer, the **eucharistic prayer**, which is a prayer of thanksgiving and praise, and which is also the prayer of blessing and consecration said over the bread and wine. (GIRM 5)

EUCHARISTIC PRAYER (1) – The central prayer of thanksgiving, praise, blessing and consecration during the celebration of the Mass. It corresponds to the BLESSING action of Jesus during the Last Supper. The eucharistic prayer is considered to be the **form** of the sacrament, with the words of Christ ("This is my body . . . this is my blood . . . ") considered essential. It was formerly subdivided into the **preface** and **canon**, and is also called the **anaphora**. Scholars suggest that the *eucharistic prayer* is descended from the **birkat ha-mazon**, a Jewish grace after meals, which is in the form of a **berakah**. The eucharistic prayer includes a proclamation of God's wonders (especially in the preface), including salvation through Jesus (especially in the **institution narrative** and **anamnesis**). It usually expresses an **offering** and contains the invocation of the Spirit in the **epiclesis** which leads to **intercessions**, and finally concludes with a **doxology**. (GIRM 54, 55)

EUCHOLOGY (3) – A term derived from the Greek word for *prayer* (εὐχή—*eukhe*). The term usually refers to a collection of prayers. A book containing prayers is sometimes called a *euchologion*.

EULOGIA (3) – Blessed pieces of bread given out after Mass. This medieval custom arose at a time of infrequent communion, possibly in imitation of the custom in the Byzantine Rite of **antidoron**. It lasted into the present century in some French-speaking areas.

EULOGY (2) – A formal speech, usually given in praise of a recently deceased individual. It was once common that funeral sermons were eulogies. However, according to the 1969 Rite of Christian Burial and the GIRM, the homily at the Mass of Christian Burial must never be a eulogy. It is permitted for a family member or friend to offer a few reflections on the deceased before the **final commendation**, however. (GIRM 338)

EVANGELARIUM (3) – Older name for the **Book of the Gospels**.

EVENING PRAYER (2) – One of the **canonical hours**, also called *vespers*. It occurs around the time of sunset. In the present Roman Rite, it consists of a hymn, psalmody (two psalms and a canticle), a reading from Scripture, the *Magnificat* (Canticle of Mary, Lk 1:46–55), intercessions and Our Father, and a final prayer and blessing. It may also be joined to the celebration of evening Mass.

EX OPERE OPERANTIS (3) – *By the action of the one acting*—a way of describing the efficacy of a sacramental action by referring to the subjective holiness of the minister of the sacrament. In traditional Catholic theology, this has been seen as secondary to *ex opere operato* efficacy.

EX OPERE OPERATO (3) – *By the action having been done*—a way of describing the efficacy of a sacramental action by referring to the objective fact of the proper ritual being performed. In traditional Catholic theology, this has been seen as the primary way of judging sacramental efficacy, but in the common estimation of many people, it tends to turn the sacraments into acts of magic in which words and actions automatically produce results regardless of the faith of the individuals involved. However, some theologians point out that *ex opere op-*

erato should be viewed as *ex opere operantis Christi*—that is, that a sacramental action ultimately depends on the action of Christ for its efficacy, and Christ has guaranteed his presence and grace, regardless of the faith and holiness of the human individuals involved.

EXCLUSIVE LANGUAGE (2) – Language that seems to exclude females, such as the generic use of "man" and "he" or "his" to mean both males and females. Recent attempts have been made to try to reword texts by using **inclusive language** so as to avoid the seeming male bias of an older style of English.

EXORCISM (3) – A prayer or command given to cast out the presence of the devil. Such a prayer still exists in the rite of infant baptism after the litany of the saints, and during the various rites of the **R.C.I.A.**

EXORCIST (3) – A **minor order** suppressed in 1972. Although all who were to be ordained priest had to receive the minor order of *exorcist*, no one was able to exercise that office without expressed delegation of the local bishop.

EXPOSITION OF THE BLESSED SACRAMENT (2) – A liturgical ceremony that includes hymns, prayers, and readings from Scripture, during which some of the reserved eucharist is removed from the tabernacle and left in a ciborium or placed in a **monstrance** for the faithful to adore. The rite may include a solemn **benediction** at its conclusion.

EXSÚLTET (2) – The solemn proclamation of the resurrection that is sung at the beginning of the Easter Vigil after the solemn procession with the Easter candle. In style, it is similar to a eucharistic prayer and includes the same initial dialogue. It is ideally sung by a deacon, and the Tridentine Missal required a priest to re-vest as a deacon if he should have to sing the *Exsúltet*. The *Exsúltet* derives its name from the first word of the Latin text (meaning *rejoice*). It is also called the **Preconium** and before the revision of the Holy Week rites in 1955 was considered to be the prayer of blessing of the Easter candle, during which it was inscribed and lighted. Tradition ascribes its authorship to **Ambrose** or **Augustine**. (GIRM 272)

EXTREME UNCTION (3) – The name used for the sacrament of the **anointing of the sick** before its revision. This title emphasized the former common practice of delaying the reception of the sacrament until the moment of death, so that it was truly the last (*extreme*) anointing (*unction*), part of the **Last Rites**.

FAITH AND ORDER (3) – Originally, a movement which worked for the unity of Christians. It was proposed by Episcopal Bishop Charles Brent in 1910, and eventually gave rise to the World Council of Churches. It started sponsoring the weeks of prayer for Christian unity in 1920 which is now celebrated during the week before the feast of the Conversion of St. Paul on January 25. The title also refers to committees of the World Council of Churches and the National Council of Churches that deal with worship.

FALDSTOOL (3) – A "folding stool" that in practice today never folds, but is used by a bishop when he is sitting, not at his **cathedra (throne)**, but in front of an altar for visibility during certain special rites.

FANON (3) – A cape-like vestment formerly worn by popes over the alb and partially over the chasuble at pontifical Masses.

FAST, EASTER (PASCHAL) (2) – The fasting associated with the sacred **triduum** of Holy Thursday, Good Friday and Holy Saturday. Technically, the Easter fast is independent from that of Lent. The **R.C.I.A.** suggests that those to be baptized at the Easter Vigil should keep the Easter fast through Good Friday and Holy Saturday until they have been baptized at the Vigil. (**Constitution on the Sacred Liturgy** 110; R.C.I.A. [1985 text] 172.1; Gen. Norms for the Liturgical Year and the Calendar 20)

FAST, EUCHARISTIC (2) – Abstaining from food and drink before the reception of communion. Presently, Catholic law prescribes that communicants should fast for one hour before receiving communion (canon 919). Medicines and water do not break the fast and the elderly and sick (and those taking care of them) are not bound by the law. Formerly, fasting from midnight was prescribed, with the result that afternoon and evening Masses were not regularly celebrated.

FAST, FRIDAY (2) – Catholic tradition and law prohibits eating meat on all Fridays (except for **solemnities**) (canon 1251). Technically, this is **abstinence** rather than *fast*, but commonly this practice is called the *Friday fast*. Since 1966, this practice can be modified by the national conferences of bishops. The United States bishops have determined that the Friday fast should be continued during Lent, but that other forms of penance may be substituted during the rest of the year. The general law of the Church also requires abstinence from meat on Ash Wednesday and Good Friday. The law of abstinence binds all those over the age of 14. The first record of the Friday fast occurs in the **Didache** (ch. 8).

FAST, LENTEN (2) – Formerly, much of Lent was a time of fasting, i.e., the reduced intake of foods. Canon law leaves the exact interpretation of this custom to national conferences of bishops, and in the United States, fasting is normally interpreted as allowing an adult to eat only one full meal. If necessary, two lesser meals that would not total another full meal may be eaten. The law of fasting presently binds those 18 to 59 and applies only on Ash Wednesday and Good Friday. (cf. canons 97, 1251, 1252)

FAST, PRE-BAPTISMAL (2) – The **Didache** (ch. 7) mentions a fast observed by a candidate for baptism and by the minister of the baptism (and by others in the community who are able) for several days prior to baptism. This seems to be the origin of the Lenten fast.

FASTING (2) – The custom of not eating food or certain foods (e.g. meat), or eating a reduced quantity of food. It is mentioned in Scripture (cf. Mt 6:16–18) and was practiced by Jesus during the 40 days in the desert after his baptism.

FEAST (2) – The second class or grade of feasts. A feast usually has a complete proper set of texts for the Mass along with readings. Feasts of Christ have three readings assigned. (GIRM 31, 315, 319)

FEASTS (2) – A common name given to celebration days in honor of Christ, Our Lady, or the saints. Feasts have been classified into three categories or ranks: **solemnities, feasts,** and **memorials.** Memorials may be *optional* or *obligatory*.

FERIA (3) – A Latin word for "weekday." It normally refers to a day on which there is no feast, and the seasonal Mass is celebrated.

FERMENTUM (3) – Formerly, the particle of eucharistic bread consecrated by the pope and taken by deacons and other ministers to various Masses held elsewhere in the city of Rome. The *fermentum* was then dropped into the cup of wine during the **commingling** as a sign of unity of the local gathering with the papal celebration.

FIBULA (3) – The ornate clasp on a **cope.**

FINAL COMMENDATION (2) – The name presently given to the farewell ritual at the end of a funeral Mass, which takes the place of the usual **concluding rite.** It consists primarily of a farewell song concluded by a prayer. It is briefly introduced, and during the song, the coffin may be sprinkled with holy water and incensed. Afterward the procession from the church to the grave takes place. This final commendation may also take place at the grave. This ritual, before its revision, was called an **absolution.** (GIRM 340)

FINGER TOWEL (2) – The cloth used by the presiding priest to dry his hands after the **washing of hands** during the preparation of the gifts. Formerly, the towel was a relatively small piece of linen, with a small red cross embroidered on the edge (to mark it differently from a **purificator**). However, since priests are no longer to wash merely their thumbs and index fingers, but their entire hands, larger (terry-cloth) hand towels are more appropriate. The *finger towel* was also called by the Latin name for a hand towel, the *manutergium,* although this word was sometimes used to refer to the **panniculus.**

FIRST FRIDAY (3) – A devotion centering around attending Mass and receiving communion on the first Friday of nine consecutive months. The devotion is associated with a promise said to have been made by Christ in an apparition to St. Margaret Mary Alacoque in the late 1600's and centers around the love of Christ through the image of the Sacred Heart. It is customary that a **votive Mass** of the Sacred Heart is said on *first Fridays.*

FIRST READING (1) – The first scriptural reading during the liturgy of the word. On Sundays and greater feast days, it is usually taken from the Hebrew Scriptures, or, during the Easter Season, from the Acts of the Apostles or Revelation. On weekdays, it may be taken either from the Hebrew Scriptures or from the writings of the apostles (other than the gospels). (GIRM 36, 89; LM 66)

FIRST SATURDAY (3) – The devotion centering around attending Mass and receiving communion on the first Saturday of five consecutive months in honor of Mary,

Mother of the Lord. This devotion grew rapidly after the apparition of Mary at Fatima in 1917.

FLABELLA (3) – Ostrich feather fans mounted on long poles which were carried around the **sedia gestatoria** when the pope was carried in procession to the altar at major papal Masses.

FOLDED CHASUBLE (3) – Formerly, folded chasubles were worn by the **deacon** and **subdeacon** at a **solemn Mass** in place of the **dalmatic** and **tunic** during penitential seasons. This was a remnant of the days when chasubles were worn by all ranks of the ordained clergy. Before the revision of the rites of ordination in the late 1960's, during a priestly ordination, a newly-ordained priest wore a folded chasuble until after communion, at which time the chasuble was unfolded to its full length. The *folded chasuble* was sometimes called a *broad stole*.

FONT, BAPTISMAL (1) – The pool or basin on a pedestal at which baptisms are celebrated. The font should be large enough so that infants may be immersed and, ideally, even adults may be able to walk into it. The ancient form was sunken with steps leading down into the pool. The water may be flowing, reminding us of Christ, the living water (Jn 4:10–14). Fonts are sometimes located in a separate structure from the main body of the church (the **baptistery**), or at a side room at the entrance of the church building (symbolic of entry into the community of believers), or at the side of the sanctuary area, so that baptisms may be celebrated during the Mass with the full participation of the assembly.

FOOTWASHING – See Washing of Feet.

FORM (2) – The text or formula that forms the major contextualizing verbal aspect of a sacrament. *Form* is frequently linked to **matter** in a description of a sacramental rite. The *form* of the eucharist has traditionally been seen as the words of Christ within a eucharistic prayer, and the *form* of baptism has been the trinitarian formula derived from the end of Matthew's gospel.

FORM, DECLARATIVE (2) – The form in which the one reciting the text makes an absolute statement, declaring something to be true. These types of texts are directed toward the people hearing them, and are not prayers to God, as in the formula for baptism in the Byzantine Rite: "The servant of God is baptized in the name of the Father . . . ." Often these forms are also in the first person indicative.

FORM, DEPRECATIVE (2) – The "prayer (*deprecatio*)" form of a liturgical text in which God is addressed directly. In the marriage rite, the last two options for blessing the rings are in deprecative form ("Lord, bless these rings which we bless in your name . . . ," "Lord, bless and consecrate . . . ").

FORM, INDICATIVE (2) – The form in which the celebrant uses "I" as in the common formula used in the Roman Rite for baptism and sacramental absolution.

FORM, INVOCATIVE (2) – The form in which God is invoked over the people, but in which the people are addressed directly. In other words, in these formulas, "you" means the people, rather than God. In the marriage rite, the first option for blessing the rings ("May the Lord bless these rings which you give to each other as the sign of your love and fidelity") may be considered to be in *invocative form*.

FORMS (Literary) OF BLESSINGS, ABSOLUTIONS, etc. (2) – The literary categories that various liturgical texts may take. The major forms are **declarative, deprecative, indicative,** or **invocative**.

FORTY HOURS (2) – An annual devotion during which the reserved sacrament is solemnly exposed for a period of about 40 hours usually over a three day period. The revised **Roman Ritual** now officially calls this devotion the *Annual Solemn* **Exposition of the Blessed Sacrament.**

FRACTION RITE (2) – Alternate name for the rite of the **breaking of the bread.**

FRONTAL (3) – An ornamental cloth, frequently matching the color (and cloth) of the chasuble, that hangs in front of the altar (and ambo) on the side visible to the assembly.

FUNERAL (2) – The name given to the rites surrounding the burial of an individual, including the vigil, Mass, and burial.

FUNERAL MASS (2) – The Mass of the dead celebrated with the body of the deceased present, immediately prior to burial. It is also called the **Mass of Christian Burial.** It should NOT be called a **Mass of Resurrection,** in order to avoid any confusion with Easter. (GIRM 336–341)

GELINEAU, JOSEPH (b. 1921) (3) – French Jesuit liturgist, particularly noted for contributing to the modern appreciation of liturgical music. He is known for composing psalm-tones that allow the psalms to be sung according to the Hebrew patterns of syllabic stresses. In English, his psalm-tones are commonly used with the **Grail** translation of the psalms (e.g. Psalm 23—"My shepherd is the Lord, nothing indeed shall I want."). He was a consultor to the commission (**Consilium**) for the revision of the Mass in the 1960's.

GENERAL INSTRUCTION OF THE LITURGY OF THE HOURS (3) – The introductory document that explains the theological background and gives the rubrical direction for celebrating the **liturgy of the hours**. In the GILH, directions are given for joining the celebration of **morning prayer** or **evening prayer** to a Mass.

GENERAL INSTRUCTION OF THE ROMAN MISSAL (3) – The introductory document that explains the theological background and gives the rubrical directions for celebrating the Mass. It forms a foundational document for any pastoral team who must prepare and plan celebrations of the Mass.

GENERAL INTERCESSIONS (1) – The prayer concluding the **liturgy of the word**. It consists of an introduction to the people by the presiding minister, various intentions read by the deacon, cantor or someone else inviting the assembly to pray, the prayer-response of the assembly, and a concluding, summary prayer by the presiding minister. In form it is a **litany**. It is also called the **prayers of the faithful** or **bidding prayers**. (GIRM 45–47)

GENUFLECTION (1) – A gesture of respect and adoration by which a person bends the right knee to touch the ground momentarily (meanwhile bending the left knee and keeping the upper body erect). It was borrowed by western Christianity from the secular gestures of respect to civil authorities. It is unknown in some monasteries and in many Eastern Churches. Formerly, a "double genuflection" was required before the blessed sacrament exposed in a monstrance, but that gesture has been discontinued. At Mass, the presiding priest genuflects toward the consecrated bread and wine after each consecration and then before inviting the assembly to receive communion. A *genuflection* is also made by all when passing in front of the tabernacle. (GIRM 233)

GESTURE (2) – Any movement of the body. The presiding priest makes numerous gestures during the liturgy, especially the **orans** gesture with his arms. Other body gestures include the laying on of hands, kissing the altar and gospel, **genuflections**, and **bows**. (cf. GIRM 20–22, 232–234)

GLORIA (1) – A song of praise sung on certain prescribed days as part of the **introductory rites** of the Mass. It is based on the hymn of the angels at Christ's birth (Lk 2:14), and was formerly used as an opening song for the Christmas Mass. (GIRM 31)

GLOVES, LITURGICAL (3) – Embroidered and jeweled gloves used to be worn by bishops while celebrating Mass until the preparation of the gifts. They are no longer mentioned in the revised liturgical books, although plain white cloth gloves are sometimes worn by the miter and crosier bearers at a formal **stational Mass**.

GODPARENT (2) – Someone who accepts responsibility for the Christian upbringing of a person who is baptized or confirmed. Sometimes the godparent is called a "sponsor" although **sponsor** also has an independent meaning of someone who vouches for the candidate. (RCIA [1985 text] 11)

GOOD FRIDAY (1) – The day on which Christ died. It is the second day of the sacred **triduum**. The liturgical service on *Good Friday* consists of the liturgy of the word with the reading of the Passion of St. John, the general intercessions in a special, solemn format, the showing and veneration of the cross, and communion from the reserved elements consecrated on Holy Thursday. It is a day of **fasting** and **abstinence**.

GOSPEL (1) – The "good news" of Jesus. Usually, *gospel* refers to one of the four accounts of the life, death and resurrection of Jesus as written by Matthew, Mark, Luke, and John. A passage from one of the four gospels is proclaimed at Mass as the last of the readings from Scripture. (GIRM 35)

GOSPEL ACCLAMATION (2) – The generic title given to the hymn welcoming the gospel proclamation, whether it be the **alleluia** or the Lenten **verse before the gospel**. Normally it consists of a refrain sung by the entire assembly, a verse (frequently from Scripture) sung by a cantor, and then the refrain again. It is a practice in some places to repeat the *gospel acclamation* after the proclamation as well.

GOSPEL BOOK – See Book of the Gospels.

The Dictionary

GOSPEL PROCESSION (2) – The common name for the short procession of the deacon (or priest who reads the gospel) with the **Book of the Gospels** (or lectionary) from the altar to the **ambo**. He may be accompanied by a thurifer and ministers with candles. During this procession the **alleluia** or **verse before the gospel** is sung. (cf. GIRM 94, 131)

GOSPEL SIDE (3) – The left side of the altar and sanctuary, as viewed from the assembly. It was the side at which a deacon sang the gospel during a solemn Mass celebrated according to the Tridentine Missal.

GRADUAL (2) – The name given in the Tridentine Missal to the **psalm** after the first reading. It was not usually in responsorial format, and originally was sung by a psalmist on a step (*gradus*) of the **ambo**. *Gradual* is also the English name of the book containing various chants for sung parts of the Mass. (GIRM 36)

GRAIL PSALMS (3) – The translation of the psalms into English by The Grail. They are frequently sung to the psalm tones of **Joseph Gelineau, S.J.**, and are the psalms used in most published versions of the **liturgy of the hours**. The translation was done conscious of the need to make the final text singable. A revised, inclusive language version appeared in 1985.

GREAT ENTRANCE (3) – The solemn transfer of the prepared bread and wine from the side table to the altar during a **Byzantine Rite** eucharistic liturgy. During the *Great Entrance*, the Cherubic Hymn is sung which is interrupted by commemorations sung by the clergy. After the Great Entrance there follows a litany, the kiss of peace, the Nicene Creed, and then the eucharistic prayer.

GREETER (2) – A minister who greets individuals as they arrive at a church for worship. In many parishes, **ushers** also perform the ministry of *greeter*. Sometimes they are called **ministers of hospitality**. (cf. GIRM 68b)

GREETING (1) – A brief, formalized dialogue usually expressing a wish of God's grace or presence to another, followed by a standardized response by the one(s) greeted. After the gathering and entrance song, the Mass continues with the presiding priest making the sign of the cross, and then *greeting* the assembly using words derived from Scripture. (GIRM 28, 86)

GREGORIAN CHANT (2) – The chant usually associated with Latin Masses and used for centuries in the Roman church. It did not employ any harmonies, and was named after Pope **Gregory the Great**.

GREGORY THE GREAT (540–604) (3) – Pope and liturgical reformer. Many prayers composed by him are found in a collection called the *Gregorian Sacramentary*. Among other achievements, he revived the practice of **stational Masses**, prescribed that the alleluia be used outside of Lent, emphasized the homily, and moved the Lord's prayer in the Roman Mass to its present location after the eucharistic prayer.

GREMIAL (2) – A (linen) napkin used by a bishop to protect the chasuble when oil is being used, e.g., at the **ordination** of priests, when the hands of the newly-ordained are anointed with **chrism**. In common practice, an **amice** is used as a gremial.

GUARDINI, ROMANO (1885–1968) (3) – Italian born liturgist who spent most of his life in Germany. Author of *The Spirit of the Liturgy* (among other books), he was one of the first to introduce the "dialogue" Mass (in Latin) in the late 1920's in his youth center, and rearranged the chapel to allow Mass facing the congregation with the congregation seated on three sides of the altar area. He held a chair at the University of Munich, which was passed on to Karl Rahner, S.J., after Guardini's death.

GUÉRANGER, PROSPER (1805–1875) (3) – Founder of the restored Benedictine Abbey at Solesmes in 1832. He is considered also the founder of the modern liturgical movement. He was the first author in modern times to use the term **paschal mystery** in liturgical writings.

HAIL MARY (2) – A common prayer, in which the first half is derived from Luke's gospel, and the second half is a traditional formula composed by the church. It is repeated as part of the **rosary**. The form used by the Roman rite is: "Hail Mary, full of grace, the Lord is with you. Blessed are you among women, and blessed is the fruit of your womb, Jesus. Holy Mary, Mother of God, pray for us, sinners, now and at the hour of our death. Amen."

HANDS, LAYING ON OF (2) – (Also called IMPOSITION OF HANDS or EXTENDING OF HANDS.) The stylized gesture of touch that is mentioned in the New Testament in conjunction with prayer (e.g. Acts 13:3; 2 Tim 1:6). Normally, both arms are outstretched over a person or object, with the palms turned downward. The same gesture is used in most of the sacraments to indicate (one of) the central, important moments, as at ordinations, or absolutions, or at the invocation of the Spirit. (Introduction to GIRM 4)

HEALING, SACRAMENTS OF (2) – A generic classification of the sacraments of **penance** and the **anointing of the sick**. Both are meant as healing sacraments: one heals the spiritual and emotional side of people, and the other heals their physical side.

HEBREW SCRIPTURES (3) – A contemporary term which is used by some authors instead of the "Old Testament." Sensitive to Jewish concerns and aware of St. Paul's insistence that "God's gifts and his call are irrevocable" (Rom 12:28–29), many suggest that it is incorrect to speak about the "Old" Testament as if it were outdated and could be ignored.

HIERARCHY (2) – Any sort of structure in which there are different levels of importance. Since there are different ranks in the church because of the sacrament of holy orders, the Church is said to be *hierarchically* arranged. However, commonly *hierarchy* refers solely to the bishops and other administrators, and sometimes they are termed *hierarchs*. (GIRM 1)

HIGH CHURCH (3) – A term given to those communities who practice a style of liturgy that emphasizes ritual and sacramental rites. The Roman Catholic and Orthodox Churches are considered the major *high churches*, along with certain segments of the Anglican communities. To distinguish themselves from high churches, some communities use the label **low church**.

HIGH MASS (3) – The common name for the form of Mass celebrated according to the Tridentine Missal, in which a priest celebrated without the assistance of a deacon or subdeacon, but in which all the prescribed parts of the Mass were sung by the priest and the people or choir. Sometimes it was called by its Latin name, *Missa Cantata* (sung Mass).

HIPPOLYTUS (3) – A Roman presbyter who lived in the first half of the third century. He was banished in 235 by the Emperor. His book of laws (*canons*) and the *Apostolic Tradition* (dated around **215**) attributed to him give us valuable information on the liturgical and ecclesial life of the early Roman church. The **eucharistic prayer** contained in the *Apostolic Tradition* lacks the **Sanctus**, but it forms the basis for the text of Eucharistic Prayer II in the present Roman Missal. Similarly, the prayer for the ordination of a bishop found in Hippolytus' *Tradition* is now used in the present Roman Pontifical. The *Tradition* seems to have been written at a time of controversy, and Hippolytus seems to be taking the traditional, orthodox position, thus reflecting an earlier tradition of liturgy, perhaps dating to the mid-second century.

HOLY FAMILY, FEAST OF THE (2) – The feast that occurs on the Sunday between Christmas and New Year's Day or on December 30 (when Christmas falls on a Sunday).

HOLY ORDERS (1) – The sacrament by which individuals are ordained for special ministry in the church as deacons, presbyters (priests), or bishops. The sacrament is conferred in an **ordination** rite through the action (**matter**) of the **imposition of hands** by a bishop on the candidate, followed by a special consecratory prayer (**form**) that is different for each order.

HOLY THURSDAY (1) – The day on which the Last Supper occurred. The Easter **triduum** is considered to begin with the evening Mass of the Lord's Supper which is celebrated on Holy Thursday. In the morning, the **chrism Mass** may also be celebrated. At the evening Mass, after the homily the **washing of feet** may be commemorated, and at the very end a special procession with bread consecrated for the Good Friday service takes place. On *Holy Thursday*, private masses are forbidden and each community is encouraged to celebrate only one Mass. (GIRM 153)

HOLY, HOLY, HOLY (2) – Sometimes-used English title for the **Sanctus**.

HOLY WEEK (2) – The week from **Passion [Palm] Sunday** to **Easter** inclusive that commemorates Christ's last days on earth, including the **paschal mystery** of his death and resurrection. In some countries and languages, the week is termed *Great Week*. (GIRM 330)

HOMILY (1) – An explanation of the scriptural readings or of the feast given by an ordained minister during a liturgy. It usually takes place after the proclamation of the gospel. It is also a reflection on the implications of Scripture and a challenge to the assembly to reform and renewal. By canonical definition (canon 767.1), the *homily* is the form of preaching given in the liturgical context by ordained ministers. If lay ministers are authorized to preach in special situations, for example, when presiding at a communion service where priests are lacking, their **preaching** may be called a *scriptural reflection* or **sermon**, but it is not technically a *homily*. (GIRM 41)

HOSPITALITY, MINISTER OF (2) – An alternate name for a **greeter** or an **usher**, particularly if the primary task is welcoming people at the doors of the church or showing hospitality afterward at some sort of social function. (GIRM 68b)

HOST (2) – The traditional name for the circular unleavened wafer bread used at the eucharist in the western churches. In the Tridentine Mass, it was common to use a larger size host (around three inches in diameter) for the priest, who would consume it all, and a smaller size (about one inch in diameter) for other members of the assembly. The GIRM now urges the use of a large enough host, so that both priest and at least some of the people may partake of the same wafer. In fact, the GIRM does not make any explicit mention of a separate host for the priest, although it says that small hosts for the people are permitted when there are large numbers. In the plural (as in "heavenly *hosts*"), the word refers to angels. (GIRM 283, 293)

HUMERAL VEIL (2) – A long veil, around two feet wide, worn over the shoulders, so that the ends could be used to carry (and cover) something precious. It is commonly worn by the priest at **benediction** or when carrying the **blessed sacrament** in a solemn procession (e.g., **Holy Thursday**). A lighter version of a humeral veil worn by the miter bearer and crosier bearer is called a **vimpa**.

HYMN (1) – A religious song, the majority of which is non-scriptural. For example, the *Gloria* is usually classified as a *hymn*, since, aside from the first sentence taken from Luke's gospel, it is a composition developed by the Christian community. Songs taken directly from Scripture (other than the **psalms**) are commonly called **canticles**. (GIRM 19)

HYPERDULIA (2) – The honor and reverence given to Mary, the Mother of God. It is above (in Greek, *hyper*) the honor given to the saints (**dulia**), but not equal to the worship properly given to God alone (**latria**).

ICON (2) – A sacred image, painted according to traditional norms, especially associated with **Byzantine Christianity**. Icons are considered to be windows into heaven, rather than mere reminders of the past. Christ is called the *icon* of the unseen God in Colossians 1:15, and the term can be applied by analogy to other things, such as the church as a whole. It is also spelled *ikon* or *eikon*.

ICONASTASIS (3) – The **icon** screen or solid wall separating the sanctuary from the body of a church in a Byzantine Church (e.g., Russian or Greek). It usually has three doorways for the clergy to pass through in the course of the liturgy: the central *Holy* or *Royal* Doors and the two side (deacon's) doors. The icon to the right of the central doorway must be that of Christ and the icon to the left of the central doors must be that of Mary.

IMMERSION, BAPTISM BY (2) – The method of administering **baptism** in which the candidate is totally immersed three times in a font or pool (stream, river). In the case of an older child or adult, the minister usually also stands in the pool and places his hand on the head of the candidate while immersing him or her and pronouncing the baptismal formula.

INCENSE (1) – Sweet-smelling resins that are burned in a **censer** on lit pieces of charcoal. According to Psalm 141:2 and Revelation 8:4, it symbolizes prayer, and is a way to respect and honor individuals and sacred objects. *Incense* is a name used both of the solid grains of resins (stored in an incense **boat**) and of the sweet-smelling smoke produced after the resin is burnt. It may be used in any Mass. (GIRM 235)

INCLUSIVE LANGUAGE (2) – Language in which the word "man" and masculine pronouns are used only to refer to males, and not used in any generic way. Reading older texts can leave the impression that women are excluded from God's love or the Church's concern, e.g., ". . . for us men and for our salvation." The problem of developing inclusive language liturgical texts and biblical translations is more pronounced in English because of the lack of a simple and traditional word to translate the Greek word *anthropos* and the Latin word *homo* in the singular (both mean "human being" without reference to gender), and to make singular pronoun references non-gender specific. Frequently, inclusive language texts render *anthropos* and *homo* in the plural as *people* or *individuals* or *human beings* or *men and women*. The term *inclusive language* is sometimes also used to refer to "God-language" that avoids the male pronoun when referring to God the Father or to the Holy Spirit.

INCULTURATION (3) – Whereas **acculturation** normally implies adaptation due to influences of a different culture (e.g. African) on the Christian forms of another culture (e.g. European), *inculturation* frequently implies a creative process wherein a new form of Christian culture is brought into being based on the local cultural heritage and the trans-cultural demands of Scripture. In a process of inculturation, some of the forms of another culture (e.g. European) may be borrowed if they blend in with the local culture (e.g. African), but the starting point is the Divine Presence and Truth that is found in the local culture, rather than that which is foreign and imported. Inculturation brings about a change in the culture through the entry of the Christian message, frequently by endowing a pre-Christian rite with Christian meaning. Both baptism and the eucharist can be viewed as prime examples of *inculturation*, since both had a pre-Christian (Jewish) meaning.

INDULGENCE (3) – Remission of effects of sin obtained through pious prayers and liturgical rites. Indulgences are now classified as either "plenary" (total) or "partial." Formerly, partial indulgences were evaluated by a specific length of time (frequently 300 or 500 days or seven years). Obtaining indulgences through almsgiving was one of **Luther's** major complaints against the Catholic Church. A plenary indulgence is sometimes granted with a papal blessing, or can be obtained by visiting a church on All Souls' Day, November 2.

INITIATION, SACRAMENTS OF (2) – The **R.C.I.A.** and other documents consider **baptism, confirmation** and the **eucharist** as the *sacraments of initiation*. The **R.C.I.A.** prescribes that previously unbaptized adults receive all three sacraments at one ceremony when being admitted into the Catholic Church. Many Orthodox Christians and Eastern Rite Catholics administer all three sacraments in one ceremony even to infants.

INSTITUTION (OF MINISTERS) (2) – The formal rite of commissioning acolytes and readers. Formerly, this was called an **ordination**, a title now reserved for deacons, presbyters (priests), and bishops. (GIRM 65–66)

INSTITUTION NARRATIVE (2) – The section of the **eucharistic prayer** in which the presiding priest narrates what the Lord did and said at the Last Supper when he instituted the eucharist. The traditional Catholic position has been that when the priest repeats the words of Christ during this section of the eucharistic prayer, the elements of bread and wine are **consecrated**. (GIRM 55d)

INTERCESSIONS, EUCHARISTIC PRAYER (2) – The section of the **eucharistic prayer** in which intercession is made for Church officials, the living and the dead, thereby showing the unity between the local community and Christians throughout the world and throughout history. It is sometimes called the **diptychs**. (GIRM 55g)

INTERCOMMUNION (2) – The reception of communion from a minister of one denomination by someone not of that denomination. The Catholic Church allows intercommunion only in very restricted situations. In general, Catholics may receive communion from Orthodox priests when Catholic priests are not accessible (and vice versa). Non-Catholics other than Orthodox may receive communion from Catholic priests only with the bishop's permission. Catholics should not receive communion from ministers of non-Orthodox non-Catholic churches. (cf. canon 844)

INTINCTION (2) – The form of distributing **communion under both kinds** in which a minister dips a particle of the consecrated bread into a cup containing the consecrated wine. Although allowed by law, it is a less than ideal form to distribute communion, since the sign value of drinking from the cup in obedience to the Lord's command has been eliminated. (GIRM 243c, 246–247)

INTRODUCTORY RITES (2) – The name given to the beginning of the Mass (or of other ceremonies). It concludes with the **opening prayer**, and is followed by the **liturgy of the word**. Normally the *introductory rites* at Mass include the entrance song, veneration of the altar, sign of the cross, greeting, penitential rite, *Kyrie*, *Gloria* and collect (i.e., opening prayer). (cf. sub-headings before GIRM 24, 82)

INTROIT (2) – The name in the Tridentine Missal given to the entrance antiphon (cf. GIRM 26). The complete *introit* consisted of the antiphon, a psalm verse, the *Glory be*, and a repetition of the antiphon.

JANSENISM (3) – The doctrines named after Cornelius Jansen (1585–1638). His doctrines were rigorous and emphasized that the human being was basically depraved in nature. It influenced piety to the extent that many people became overly aware of sin and absented themselves from frequent communion.

JEROME (345–420) (3) – Translator of the Bible from Greek into Latin (the *Vulgate* translation). In his commentary on Paul's letter to the Galatians, he says that the "Amen" at the end of the eucharistic prayer thundered in Rome and caused the pagan temples to tremble (*In Epist. ad Gal.* 2, pref., Migne's *Patrologia Latina* 26:381).

JOHN XXIII (1881–1963) (3) – Born Angelo Roncalli, elected pope in 1958. He convened the Second Vatican Council, but died before the Council issued its **Constitution on the Sacred Liturgy**. He is considered to be the originator of the updating movement in the Catholic Church.

JOHN CHRYSOSTOM (347–407) (3) – Patriarch of Constantinople and, along with **Basil**, Gregory the Theologian (Nazianzen), and Athanasius, one of the four great Greek doctors of the Church. Many of his sermons are preserved, some of which give us an insight into the liturgical theology of his day. He is quoted as supporting the position that the words of Christ in the eucharistic prayer transform the elements: "The priest acts as the representative of Christ when he pronounces those words . . . 'This is my Body' he says. These words transform the offerings before him." (*In proditione Judae.*, Hom. 1:6, Migne's *Patrologia Graeca* 49:380)

JUNGMANN, JOSEF ANDREAS (1889–1975) (3) – Austrian Jesuit liturgist. Among other works, he authored *The Mass of the Roman Rite*, one of the first detailed, historical analyses of the structure and origins of the rituals in the Mass. He also worked on the 1960's revision of the Mass as a consultor to the **Consilium**.

JUSTIN (c. 100-c. 165) (3) – Roman martyr, born in Syria, converted to Christianity around 130. His *Dialogue with Trypho* and his *First Apology* give us the earliest description of a eucharistic celebration. He speaks of the blessed food as the "eucharist" and that they are not "ordinary" bread and wine, but the "flesh and blood of that incarnate Jesus" (66:1–2). He mentions the prayer of "praise and glory" offered to God by the "presider" after which "all the people present give their assent by saying: Amen" (65:3).

KENOSIS (3) – The *emptying out* of Jesus in becoming a member of the human race (cf. Phil 2:7). This self-emptying is remembered in the liturgy in that the assembly celebrates its union with Christ and its willingness to give of itself for the sake of others. (cf. GIRM 55f)

KISS (2) – A *kiss* is the normal form of reverence toward the altar (after an initial bow) upon arriving in the sanctuary at the end of the entrance procession. It is made by deacons, presbyters, and bishops, but not by assisting ministers. At the end of Mass, the presiding priest and the deacon (if present), but not any concelebrants, *kiss* the altar if it is convenient. The gospel text is also kissed after its proclamation. On Good Friday, the cross may be kissed during its veneration. Formerly, other liturgical objects were kissed according to the rubrics associated with the Tridentine Missal. (GIRM 27, 95, 125, 131, 141, 208, 232)

KISS OF PEACE (3) – An older term for the **Sign of Peace** (cf. 2 Cor 13:12).

KNEELER (2) – A stand with a (padded) step at which someone can kneel and (usually) place a book for prayer or reading. It is also called a **prie-dieu**.

KNEELING (1) – The body posture in which both knees touch the ground (or rest on a **prie-dieu**). This is a common posture for private prayer in the western church, and is especially appropriate during penitential times. The Council of Nicaea in 325 forbade kneeling on Sundays and during the Easter season (Nicaea canon 20). At Mass, the assembly usually kneels during part of the eucharistic prayer. (GIRM 21)

KOINONIA (3) – The Greek word for *communion*. It is particularly used in reference to a unity between individuals fostered and celebrated in common worship. In Acts 4:42, we read that the early Christians devoted themselves to "*koinonia*, the **breaking of the bread**, and prayer."

KYRIE (2) – Vocative case of *Κύριος, Kyrios*, a Greek word meaning *Lord* or *Master*. When the Old Testament was translated into Greek, *Kyrios* was the word used to translate the Hebrew words *Adonai* ("my lord") or *Yahweh* ("I am who am"—Ex 3:14), the name used for God in the Hebrew Scriptures. In Philippians 2:11, Paul quotes a hymn that proclaims: "Jesus Christ is *Kyrios* to the glory of God the Father." In the liturgy,

Kyrie, eleison originally was the response to a litany similar to the present **general intercessions**. It now forms a short litany addressed to Christ, and is part of the **introductory rites** that precede the liturgy of the word. (GIRM 30)

LAITY, PRIESTHOOD OF THE (2) – The term used to refer to the priesthood that all Christians receive as a result of their baptism. Because of this priesthood, they truly offer sacrifice to God through their lives and their prayers (cf. 1 Pet 2:5,9). This is usually distinguished from the *ministerial priesthood* conferred on individuals through the sacrament of **holy orders**. (cf. GIRM 62)

LAMB (3) – The name given in the **Byzantine Rite** to the large square piece of bread carved by the priest during the preparation rite at the **prothesis** and consecrated for communion.

LAMB OF GOD (2) – The English name for the **Agnus Dei**, sung during the **breaking of the bread**.

LANGUAGE, EXCLUSIVE – See Exclusive Language.

LANGUAGE, INCLUSIVE – See Inclusive Language.

LANGUAGE, LATIN (2) – The traditional language used in worship by the **Roman Rite** of the Catholic Church. Even today, liturgical books are first issued in Latin and then translated into other languages. Latin is encouraged for hymns used at multi-lingual and multi-ethnic gatherings. (cf. GIRM 19)

LANGUAGE, LITURGICAL (2) – The language used for liturgy. Before the Second Vatican Council, Latin and Glagolitic were the only liturgical languages for **Roman Rite** Catholics. Koine Greek and Old Slavonic were frequently used as liturgical languages in the **Byzantine Rite**. Liturgical languages before the Council were either dead languages or older forms of contemporary languages, but not the commonly used language.

LANGUAGE, SEXIST (2) – Language that uses male nouns and pronouns in a generic way to exclude women. There is a contemporary trend that tries to use **inclusive language** wherever it is possible to avoid *sexist language*.

LANGUAGE, VERNACULAR (2) – The common language of the people used in the geographical area. Vernacular need not be slang or jargon, but merely the standard (polite) language of the local people. (cf. Introduction to GIRM 11–13)

LAPPETS (3) – The two pieces of cloth, around two inches wide and eight inches long, that hang from the back of a **miter**.

LAST GOSPEL (3) – The selection from the beginning of St. John's Gospel (1:1–14) that was read in the **Tridentine Mass** *after* the dismissal and blessing.

LAST RITES (3) – Formerly, the sacraments given to a person near death, usually in the order: **penance, viaticum,** and **extreme unction**, followed by a papal blessing for the dying. The contemporary understanding suggests that the anointing of the sick should be given to someone earlier in an illness and *the* last rites should merely be penance and viaticum. If the anointing takes place, viaticum should always *follow* it as *the* last sacrament.

LAST SUPPER (2) – The last meal Jesus shared with his apostles, on the night before he died. This meal is mentioned in the gospels (Mt 26:19 ff., Mk 14:16 ff., Lk 22:13 ff., Jn 13:1 ff.) and in Paul (1 Cor 11:23). Matthew, Mark and Luke describe it as a Passover meal, but John suggests that it was celebrated on the night before Passover started. In Matthew, Mark, Luke and Paul, we read about the institution of the **eucharist**, and in John we read about the **washing of feet**. In some Christian churches, the eucharist is commonly called a *Last Supper* service. (GIRM 48)

LATRIA (2) – Adoration properly due to God alone or to one of the persons of the Trinity. It is distinguished from **dulia** and **hyperdulia**, which are the honor and praise given to the saints and to the Blessed Virgin Mary, respectively.

LAUDS (2) – The older name used for **morning prayer**, one of the **canonical hours**.

LAVÁBO (3) – The name sometimes given to the **washing of hands** at Mass. It is derived from the section of Psalm 26 (verses 6–12) prescribed to be said during the washing in the Tridentine Missal (*Lavábo inter innocéntes manus meas: et circúmdabo altáre tuum, Dómine: . . .*). The revised Missal uses a different text, taken from Psalm 51 (*Lava me, Dómine, . . .*), but the older name continues to be used.

LAVANAUX, MAURICE (1893–1974) (3) – Founder of the Liturgical Arts Society (in 1928) and its only secretary. He was the editor of *Liturgical Arts* magazine, a key periodical in the updating of art forms to the demands of a contemporary liturgy. Unfortunately, the Society disbanded in 1972 and the magazine ceased publication.

LECTERN (2) – The reading stand used for proclaiming the word of God at the **ambo**. (GIRM 272)

LECTIO CONTINUA (2) – The *continuous reading* of Scripture at Mass and in the office of readings in the liturgy of the hours. It was an ancient tradition to read from Scripture in a continuous or semi-continuous manner, beginning one day at the point where the previous day's reading ended. This tradition is followed for the most part in the Sunday and weekday lectionary cycles. (cf. GIRM 319)

LECTIONARY (1) – The book containing all the scriptural readings proclaimed at Mass, along with the responsorial psalms. However, the gospels may be contained in a separate **Book of the Gospels**. The revised Lectionary of 1969 returned to an older practice of assigning specific readings to each day of the year. In the Tridentine Missal, only Sundays, major feasts, and Lenten weekdays had assigned readings. The *Introduction to the Lectionary* was revised in 1981. (GIRM 80b)

LECTOR (2) – An alternate name for the **reader**, derived from the Latin.

LENT (1) – The penitential period of preparation before the celebration of Christ's death and resurrection during the sacred **triduum**. It is approximately 40 days long, imitating the 40 days of prayer and fasting of Jesus in the desert after his baptism. In the western church, it begins on **Ash Wednesday**, and continues for six weeks. In the Byzantine Rite, it begins two days earlier, on the Monday prior to the First Sunday of Lent. It ends with the evening Mass of the Lord's Supper on **Holy Thursday**. The last week of Lent, which begins with the sixth Sunday, **Passion [Palm] Sunday**, is called **Holy Week**. In the Tridentine Missal, there was a pre-Lenten period which began with **Septuagesima Sunday**. (Gen. Norms for the Liturgical Year and the Calendar, 28)

LEONINE PRAYERS (AFTER MASS) (3) – The prayers formerly prescribed to be said after **low Mass**. They consisted of three Hail Mary's, the Hail Holy Queen, two prayers, and three invocations to the Sacred Heart. Their use was discontinued in 1964. An early version of these prayers was ordered by Pope Pius IX in 1859 in areas affected by the collapse of the papal states. With the German *Kulturkampf* in mind, Pope Leo XIII in 1884 added a prayer and ordered that they be said throughout the world. Pius X added the final invocations in 1904 and Pius XII in 1934 prescribed that they be said for the conversion of Russia.

LEX ORANDI, LEX CREDENDI (3) – *The Law of Praying, The Law of Believing*. This is a standard maxim and may be quoted in one of several forms. It indicates the interconnection of worship and faith. (cf. Introduction to GIRM, 2)

LIBER USUALIS (3) – A book of chants that contains the official Gregorian melodies for all the proper antiphons of the Mass and the **divine office**, and various Gregorian melodies for the ordinary parts of the Tridentine Mass. In addition, it includes the text of the scriptural readings for Mass and the canonical hours. The common edition of the *Liber Usualis* was edited by the Benedictine monks of **Solesmes**. It was a book in common use in seminaries and monasteries whenever the divine office or Mass was sung according to traditional Gregorian melodies.

LIGHTS, PROCESSIONAL (2) – Candles, usually in special holders, carried by ministers in procession. (cf. GIRM 82b)

LITANY (2) – A form of prayer in which a standard response is given to numerous variable invocations. The **general intercessions** and the **Agnus Dei** are both litanies in their form. The **Kyrie** seems to be the response to a litany that disappeared somewhere in history. At the Easter Vigil, the Litany of the Saints is prayed as part of the rite of Christian initiation.

LITURGICAL ARCHITECTURE – See Architecture, Liturgical.

LITURGICAL ART – See Art, Liturgical.

LITURGICAL MOVEMENT (2) – The movement whose goal is the authentic celebration of liturgy and the proper integration of Christian life with worship. The modern movement began in France in 1832 with the refounding of the Benedictine abbey of **Solesmes** by Dom **Prosper Guéranger**, and received a fresh start in 1909 with an address given at the National Congress of

Catholic Works, in Malines, Belgium, by Dom **Lambert Beauduin**, who called for vernacular Missals for the people.

LITURGICAL MUSIC TODAY (3) – A 1982 statement of the U.S. National Conference of Catholic Bishops updating the earlier statement, **Music in Catholic Worship**.

LITURGY (1) – From a Greek word meaning *work of the people*. It refers to any official form of public worship. In the eastern churches, the Mass is often called the *Divine Liturgy*. The title is frequently used in conjunction with a modifier, such as the *liturgy of the hours*, the *liturgy of the eucharist*, etc.

LITURGY COMMITTEE (2) – A group of individuals charged with assisting the presiding priests and the local assembly in preparing for and planning liturgical celebrations. The tasks of these committees vary from locale to locale, but besides suggesting the music to be used, they may also help prepare the environment for worship, and determine the degree of solemnity used, thus determining the appropriateness of certain options (e.g. incense).

LITURGY OF THE EUCHARIST (1) – The section of the Mass that begins after the **general intercessions** and ends with the **prayer after communion**. It has a four-fold biblically-based structure: TAKE, BLESS, BREAK, SHARE. After the TAKING and preparation of the bread and wine, the BLESSING is pronounced through the **eucharistic prayer**, followed by the **Lord's Prayer** and **sign of peace**. This is followed by the BREAKING OF THE BREAD and the SHARING of the consecrated elements in **communion**. (GIRM 8, 48–56)

LITURGY OF THE HOURS (1) – The daily official liturgical prayer of the church, by which the various times of the day are sanctified. Its celebration is tied in with the various *hours* of the day. It is also called the **canonical hours**, **divine office** or **breviary**.

LITURGY OF THE WORD (1) – The section of the Mass that follows the **introductory rites**, and consists of several readings from Scripture followed by a **homily**, the **profession of faith** (if prescribed), and the **general intercessions**. On Sundays and major feasts, three readings are prescribed, while on weekdays only two. The readings follow this order: **first reading**, **responsorial psalm**, **second reading**, **alleluia**, **gospel**. (GIRM 8, 33–47)

LORD (2) – A biblical and liturgical title now used for any person of the Trinity. In the **Gloria**, God is addressed as *Lord God, Heavenly King*, and Jesus is addressed as *Lord Jesus Christ*. In the **Nicene Creed**, the Holy Spirit is said to be the *Lord and Giver of Life*. Jewish tradition prohibits pronouncing the sacred name of God, *Yahweh*, and instead *Adonai* is spoken in Hebrew, or *Kyrios* in Greek (see entry for **Kyrie** above), which is rendered into English as *Lord*. That title for God was transferred to Jesus in the Christian era and has been used in the liturgy from early days.

LORD'S DAY (2) – An alternate name for **Sunday**. It was used as early as in the **Didache** (ch. 14).

LORD'S PRAYER (1) – The prayer taught by Jesus to his disciples. Although two forms appear in the gospels, a longer form in Matthew 6:9–13 and a shorter form in Luke 11:2–4, the Church has regularly used an adaptation of Matthew's form, which also appears in the **Didache** (ch. 8) with minor changes. In the Roman Mass, the *Lord's Prayer* follows the eucharistic prayer and precedes the prayer for peace (having been moved there by **Gregory the Great**). The final **doxology** (*For the kingdom, . . .*) appears in the *Didache* and some manuscripts of Matthew, and is now in common use in the Roman Rite, the Byzantine Rite, and other Rites. However, in the Tridentine Mass this doxology was not used. In the Roman Mass, an **embolism** of the last petition is prayed by the priest between the text of the prayer and its doxology. (GIRM 56a)

LORD'S SUPPER (2) – An alternate name for the Mass that particularly recalls its connection to the **Last Supper**. It is taken from 1 Corinthians 11:20. (GIRM 2, 7)

LOW CHURCH (3) – A term given to those communities who practice a style of liturgy that emphasizes the word and preaching, and uses a minimum of ritual or sacramental rites. Some segments of the Anglican community style themselves as *low church*. A contrasting term is **high church**.

LOW MASS (3) – The common form of Mass celebrated according to the Tridentine Missal. There was no singing by the priest, and all responses were said by the altar servers. Sometimes the people or choir did sing hymns during a low Mass, but that singing was not considered to be a part of the necessary texts of the Mass.

LOW SUNDAY (3) – The name formerly given in English to the Sunday after Easter, because of the contrast to the Easter celebration on the previous weekend. In Latin, the title was *Dominica in albis* ("Sunday in white"), referring to the white garments that the newly-baptized wore for the last time on that day. It was also called *Quasimodo Sunday*, from the first word of the Latin **Introit** (*"Just as* newborn babes . . .).

LUNETTE (2) – The container with glass sides that holds a large **host** and is placed in a **monstrance** for solemn **exposition of the blessed sacrament**.

LUTHER, MARTIN (1483–1546) (3) – Father of the Protestant Reformation. In 1517, he posted his 95 theses on the church door in Wittenberg. Some of his criticisms of the Catholic practices of his day were against liturgical practices. As a result, he translated the Mass texts into the vernacular in 1526 and began distributing communion under both kinds. Because of the objections raised by Luther and his followers, the Council of Trent tried to correct some abuses but reiterated the validity of the Church's established practices (e.g., the use of Latin, communion under one kind), some of which were not changed until the Second Vatican Council.

LUTHERAN BOOK OF WORSHIP (3) – The service book used by Lutherans. A peculiarity of the Lutheran eucharistic liturgy is the eucharistic prayer, which according to Lutheran tradition, consists of a **preface, Sanctus**, and then the **institution narrative**. The recently revised books of worship do include alternate eucharistic prayers following a more traditional style.

MAJOR ORDERS (3) – The sacramental ranks of ministry derived from **holy orders**, namely **deacon, priest**, and **bishop**. Before its suppression, **subdeacon** was considered a *major order*, although most theologians considered it non-sacramental.

MANDATUM (2) – A name sometimes given to the rite of **washing the feet** on Holy Thursday. The name is Latin for *commandment* and is the first word of John 13:34 in the Latin text ("I give you a new commandment"), a verse similar in style and content to John 13:15 where Jesus explains the meaning behind his action of washing their feet ("I . . . give you an example").

MANIPLE (3) – A vestment used before 1967 that was worn around the left forearm by bishops, priests, deacons and subdeacons. It had its origin in a towel draped over the arm.

MARIA LAACH (3) – A Benedictine monastery in Rhineland, Germany, home of Dom **Odo Casel**. It was there and at **Solesmes** that much of the early liturgical renewal in the late nineteenth and early twentieth centuries took place.

MARIAN DEVOTIONS (2) – Devotions to Mary, the mother of Jesus. These include public recitation of the rosary, crowning of statues, especially during the month of May, and processions.

MARIAN MONTH (2) – The month of May, dedicated to Mary, known for **marian devotions**.

MARRIAGE (1) – The permanent union of man and woman in a companionship of love. Natural marriage comes from God and is divinely blessed, but the marriage of two baptized Christians is considered a **sacrament**, the sacrament of **matrimony**.

MARTYR (2) – Someone who dies, usually at the hands of non-Christians or non-Catholics, because of his or her allegiance to Christ. There are saints who have died a violent death who are not considered martyrs, because the death was due to a non-religious dispute (e.g., Joan of Arc). (GIRM 308b)

MASS (1) – The name for the entire eucharistic celebration of the Roman Rite. It is derived from the Latin word for dismissal, *missa*. (GIRM 1)

MASS OF CHRISTIAN BURIAL (2) – The official title for the **funeral Mass**, said with the body present, immediately before the procession to the cemetery for burial. At the end of this Mass, the **final commendation** takes place. (cf. GIRM 340)

MASS OF THE CATECHUMENS (3) – The title given in the Tridentine Missal to the first half of the Mass, from the entrance procession and **prayers at the foot of the altar**, up to (and including) the **creed**. It was so named because, according to ancient tradition, the **catechumens** were dismissed at its conclusion, a practice that has been revived in the **R.C.I.A.**

MASS OF THE FAITHFUL (3) – The title given in the Tridentine Missal to the second half of the Mass, from the **offertory** to the **last gospel**.

MASS OF THE PRE-SANCTIFIED (3) – The title formerly given to the Good Friday liturgy. A similar title is still used for the special combined vespers and communion service held during Lent in the Byzantine Rite. The word *pre-sanctified* indicates that there is no consecration during the service, but that the eucharistic bread that is distributed had been consecrated at a eucharist celebrated earlier in the week.

MASS OF THE RESURRECTION (2) – Technically, this refers only to the Easter Vigil Mass and the Masses celebrated during Easter day. This title is sometimes used to refer to the **funeral Mass** or the **Mass of Christian Burial**, based on the argument that the funeral Mass celebrates the resurrection of the deceased to a new life with Christ. However, the double use of *resurrection* leads to confusion and ambiguity and is officially discouraged.

MASTER OF CEREMONIES (2) – The person who directs the presiding priest and other ministers, particularly at more solemn services, and insures that the service is carried out properly and with decorum. (cf. GIRM 69)

MATRIMONY (2) – The sacrament of **marriage**. Before the Second Vatican Council, the sacrament was celebrated before the beginning of the **nuptial Mass**, and marriages between a Catholic and a non-Catholic were not permitted to be celebrated in a Church (they were usually performed in the sacristy or the rectory). As a result of the **Constitution on the Sacred Liturgy** 78, the rite of marriage now takes place during the liturgy of the word after the homily, and marriages between Catholics and non-Catholics may even take place during a Mass (although many consider a non-eucharistic service more appropriate).

MATTER (2) – The physical material and the gestures that together form the major visible aspect of a sacrament. *Matter* is frequently linked to **form** in describing a sacramental rite. The *matter* of the eucharist has traditionally been seen as the wheat bread and grape wine, and the *matter* of baptism has been the washing with water (either by pouring over the head or by total immersion).

MAUNDY THURSDAY (3) – An old English name for **Holy Thursday**, derived from a title for the rite of **washing the feet**, the **mandatum**.

MAY, MONTH OF (2) – The month dedicated to Mary, the mother of Jesus, and sometimes called the **Marian month**.

McMANUS, FREDERICK (b. 1923) (3) – American liturgist and canonist. Former dean of the School of Canon Law at the Catholic University of America and former director of the U.S. Bishops' Committee on the Liturgy, he was one of the few Americans who served as a consultor to the post-conciliar commission (**Consilium**) that revised the Mass.

MEAL (2) – Since the core of the **eucharist** involves bread and wine that have been blessed and then received as sacred food, the eucharist is rightly called a *meal*, recalling the numerous meals Jesus shared and hosted for people, particularly the **Last Supper**. It is also seen as a preview of the eternal banquet depicted in Scripture as occurring in heaven. (GIRM 241, cf. GIRM 240)

MEDIATOR DEI (3) – The encyclical letter promulgated by Pope Pius XII in 1947 that gave official support and encouragement to the **liturgical movement**. It encouraged the practice of distributing hosts consecrated at that Mass to those who wished to receive communion, rather than using hosts previously consecrated and taken from the tabernacle.

MEMORIAL (2) – A common way of translating **anamnesis**. The word has suffered from polemical arguments over the years. Some (mainly non-Catholics) term the eucharist a *memorial* to distinguish it from **sacrament**, and they see the Mass as equivalent to any memorial ceremony, for example, one remembering those who died in a war. Others (mainly Catholics and Orthodox) see in the term *memorial* the *active remembering and presence* that is conveyed by the word *anamnesis*. *Memorial* is also the term used to describe the third rank of **feasts** of the calendar. Memorials themselves may be classified as either *obligatory* or *optional*. During privileged seasons (e.g. Lent), all memorials are considered optional and are observed, if desired, only by use of the special **collect** at Mass. (GIRM 7, 55e, 315, 316)

MEMORIAL ACCLAMATION (2) – The acclamation made by the assembly during the **eucharistic prayer** after the **institution narrative** and the invitation, "Let us proclaim the mystery of faith." The Latin gives three possible texts, the first of which has been translated into English in two different ways. Each acclamation refers to the **paschal mystery** and the second coming. (GIRM 17a)

The Dictionary 149

METAPHOR (2) – A figure of speech containing a comparison, usually implied. In a metaphor, a word or phrase that is normally used in one context is applied to something totally different, without the use of comparison words such as *as* or *like*. The *Body of Christ* is a metaphor applied to the Christian community.

METHODISM (3) – Referring to the method of worship and the doctrines of the Methodists. The Methodists developed from the work and teachings of John and Charles Wesley in the early eighteenth century in the United States. The Wesleys were devout Episcopalians whose followers were characterized by methodical study and worship. A particular Methodist form of worship is the **Covenant service**.

MICHEL, VIRGIL (1888–1938) (3) – Benedictine monk of St. John's Abbey in Collegeville, Minnesota. He was founder and first editor of *Worship* magazine (first titled *Orate Fratres*). Later, this work gave rise to the establishment of the *Liturgical Press*. A tireless worker, he believed that good liturgy was not the preserve of monasteries, and campaigned to unite liturgy and life, ritual and social justice.

MIMESIS (3) – Imitation or mimicry.

MINISTER (1) – Anyone who serves ("ministers to") the worshipping community by exercising some ministry. The ordained clergy are sometimes called *sacred ministers*, but others who perform a liturgical function may also be called ministers. Some of the more common liturgical ministers are: reader, acolyte, usher, choir, cantor, and server. (GIRM 58–73)

MINISTER OF HOSPITALITY – See **Hospitality, Minister of.**

MINISTER, EUCHARISTIC (2) – Anyone who ministers communion, under the form of bread or of wine. Usually, the name is applied to the laity, although the title can also be applied to priests and deacons.

MINISTER, EXTRAORDINARY (2) – A literal translation of the Latin *minister extraordinarius*, referring to those who are authorized to distribute communion and have not been ordained as deacons, priests, or bishops. An alternate English title is **special minister**.

MINISTER, ORDINARY (2) – Those who by their ordination as deacons, priests, or bishops have the ordinary duty, as part of their office in the church, to minister communion at the eucharist.

MINISTER, SPECIAL (2) – Those who are authorized to distribute communion and have not been ordained as deacons, priests, or bishops. They are usually commissioned with the permission of the local bishop, either in a common ceremony, or for a given occasion according to a brief rite found in one of the appendices of the sacramentary. An alternate English title is **extraordinary minister**. (GIRM 65)

MINISTER TO THE SICK (2) – A **eucharistic minister** whose primary responsibility is to visit the sick, pray with them offering spiritual consolation, and bring them communion.

MINOR ORDERS (3) – The non-sacramental ranks of ministry instituted by the Church. In the Roman Church, prior to the 1972 revision, the minor orders were those of **porter, exorcist, reader,** and **acolyte**. They were conferred by a rite of **ordination**. After the revision, the *minor orders* are called *minor ministries* and are only **reader** and **acolyte**.

MISSA PRO POPULO (3) – The Mass said by bishops of dioceses and pastors of parishes for the people entrusted to their care. A *missa pro populo* is required to be celebrated each Sunday and holy day of obligation. (canons 388, 534)

MISSAL, ROMAN (2) – The general title for the book or books containing the prayers, hymns, and scriptural readings prescribed for the celebration of Mass. The Council of Trent ordered the revision of the Mass which resulted in the *Roman Missal* of 1570, also called the *Tridentine Missal*. The Second Vatican Council ordered another revision of the Mass which resulted in the Missal of 1970. Before Trent, the various texts were found in different books, but these were combined into one volume after the Council. The one volume Missal was commonplace until the Second Vatican Council. Nowadays, the Missal is subdivided into the book of prayers used by the priest or **sacramentary**, the book containing the scriptural readings or **lectionary**, and the book of hymns and antiphons or **gradual**. (Introduction to GIRM 6–7)

MISSALETTE (2) – The (usually disposable) leaflet booklets for the use of the faithful containing some of the texts used at Mass. It often contains the readings and some hymns as well. A number of authors suggest that *missalettes* are a mixed blessing and may actually be detrimental to good liturgy. Although helpful for those hard of hearing or unfamiliar with the Mass, for many people they inhibit participation rather than encourage it. Those who go to a play do not read the script during the performance, yet most missalettes are merely copies of the "script" for Mass. (cf. LM 37)

MITER (2) – The hat used by a bishop as a sign of his office. In the west, the miter is pointed, has two **lappets,** and is so made that when not worn it lies flat. In the Byzantine Rite, the miter is shaped like an imperial crown. The miter may also be worn by certain priests as a sign of their office, e.g. abbots, protonotaries apostolic, mitered archpriests. In the west, those who wear a miter, also wear a **zucchetto** under it. The miter need not be worn at every Mass, but it is normally worn at the more solemn ceremonies. In the Roman Rite, it is worn during processions, when seated, and at solemn absolutions, invocations or blessings. It may also be worn during the homily. It is not worn while praying or during the proclamation of the gospel.

MIXED CHALICE (2) – The cup containing both water and wine. Several ancient liturgical texts refer to a *mixed* chalice rather than merely a cup of wine. The mixture of water and wine is a symbol of Christ who in his person united the divine (wine) with the human (water).

MONSTRANCE (2) – The vessel used to display a large consecrated **host** during **exposition of the blessed sacrament.** It frequently has the shape of a large cross with a base so that it can stand upright on a flat surface. At the juncture of the two sections, there is a clear round window for the **lunette** with the host to be placed. Older styles have jeweled rays streaming forth from the window. (GIRM 292)

MORNING PRAYER (2) – One of the **canonical hours** of the **liturgy of the hours**, also known by the older name of **lauds**. Ideally, it is prayed at sunrise and may be joined to Mass according to norms found in the **General Instruction of the Liturgy of the Hours**. In the present Roman Rite, it consists of a hymn, psalmody (two psalms and a canticle), a reading from Scripture, the *Benedictus* (Canticle of Zechariah, Lk 1:68–79), intercessions and Our Father, and a final prayer and blessing. Along with **evening prayer**, it forms one of the "hinges" on which the liturgy of the hours turns (cf. Constitution on the Sacred Liturgy, 89a).

MORSE (3) – The ornate clasp on a **cope**. Also called a **formale**, or a **fibula**.

MOVEMENT, LITURGICAL – See **liturgical movement**.

MUSIC (1) – Ancient liturgical texts seem to presuppose the presence of music and song at worship services. It is still customary in some parts of the world always to sing at Mass, and never to celebrate the eucharist without song. Recent decrees on music emphasize that it is the *handmaid* of the liturgy, in that it is integral to the worship taking place and not merely an end in itself. The music used to sustain the singing should be simple enough that the entire assembly may be able to sing and not be discouraged because of the complexity of the compositions. (cf. GIRM 19)

MUSIC IN CATHOLIC WORSHIP (3) – The 1972 statement of the U.S. National Conference of Catholic Bishops regarding the use of **music**. It is an attempt to expand on the suggestions found in GIRM 14–19 and elsewhere, and give additional guidelines based on the literary characteristics of English. A supplementary statement, entitled **Liturgical Music Today**, was issued in 1982 on the tenth anniversary of the original statement. In 1983, the original statement was amended slightly and reissued.

MUSICIAN (2) – Anyone who ministers to the assembly by accompanying the singing with musical instruments. (GIRM 63)

MUST (3) – Freshly squeezed grape juice that has just begun the fermentation process. In cases of necessity or by indult, *must* may be used at Mass in the place of **wine**.

MYSTAGOGICAL CATECHESIS (2) – The post-baptismal instruction given to the newly-baptized, especially during the Easter season. The name is first found in the writings of **Cyril of Jerusalem**.

MYSTAGOGY (2) – The process of receiving the post-baptismal instruction called **mystagogical catechesis**. It is a part of the **R.C.I.A.**, normally coinciding with the Easter season.

MYSTERY (2) – Something or someone that is unknown and perhaps unknowable. God is said to be a *mystery* since the Trinity is unknowable in its totality by human beings. Paul speaks about the gospel revealing the *mystery* hidden for all ages (Rom 16:25). Especially in

Greek writings, the sacraments are called *mysteries*, and the Mass is sometimes called the *Sacred Mysteries*.

MYTH (3) – A story that may or may not be based on historical fact, and that conveys a belief, or explains a practice or natural phenomenon. Certain important biblical passages are myth, such as the creation story in Genesis, but still proclaim a religious truth.

NARRATIVE (3) – A literary form, in which the text narrates a story. Part of the eucharistic prayer is called the **institution narrative** since it narrates what Jesus said and did at the Last Supper.

NARTHEX (2) – The section of a church building between the main doors and the main seating section for the assembly (i.e., the **nave**). Also called the porch or **vestibule**.

NAVE (2) – The main section of a church building where the assembly gathers for worship. It is the section usually containing the **pews** for the people and is distinct from the **sanctuary** area.

NEOPHYTE (2) – A newly baptized Christian.

NICENE CREED (2) – The standard form of the **profession of faith** used at Mass. It was first approved at the Council of Nicaea in 325.

NIGHT PRAYER (2) – The last office of the **liturgy of the hours**, also known by its older name, **compline**. It is said usually right before bedtime. It normally consists of an examination of conscience, followed by one or two psalms, a verse of Scripture, a responsory, the *Nunc Dimittis* (Canticle of Simeon, Lk 2:29–32), and concludes with a prayer, blessing, and hymn to Mary.

NOVENA (2) – A devotion that is celebrated for nine days, which sometimes precedes a feast. It usually consists of special prayers and public liturgies. In the days before evening Masses were permitted, if people attended non-eucharistic services in church in the evening, the services were frequently related to novenas.

NUPTIAL BLESSING (2) – The special blessing imparted to a newly-married couple at their marriage. Traditionally, the blessing takes the place of the **embolism** and **doxology** of the **Lord's prayer**. Formerly, it was construed as a special blessing of the bride, and could only be given once. Thus, if a widow were to re-marry, she could not be given the nuptial blessing again. That restriction has been dropped in the revised (1969) marriage rite.

NUPTIAL MASS (2) – The wedding Mass, during which the rite of **marriage** takes place and the **nuptial blessing** is given.

OBJECTS, LITURGICAL (2) – A generic name given to all material objects used during liturgies. EACW emphasizes that quality, authenticity, and beauty should be aspects of all liturgical objects (EACW 20, 34, 36, 67) and that minimalism has no place in the contemporary liturgy (EACW 14, 15).

OBLIGATION, HOLY DAY OF (2) – Days on which Catholics are obliged to worship God by attending Mass. Present Roman Catholic law prescribes Sundays and ten solemnities as days of obligation, but only six of these solemnities are observed in the United States, and two in Canada. (canons 1246-7)

OCTAVE (2) – The eight day period during which a feast is celebrated. It consists of the feast day itself and seven days following the feast. In the revised Missal, only two feasts have octaves: Christmas and Easter. (GIRM 316a, 330)

OFFERING (2) – In the revised Missal, *offering* or *offer* is used only to describe the section of the **eucharistic prayer** that occurs after the institution narrative and **anamnesis** and contains the words "we offer." This is the point at which the only true offering takes place, with the assembly joining Christ in the once for all perfect offering of himself to God (Heb 7:27). (GIRM 55f)

OFFERING, MASS (2) – The title given by the 1983 Code of Canon Law to the monetary donation given to a priest with the understanding that Mass will be celebrated. The Latin word now used is *stips*, whereas the Latin word used in the 1917 Code of Canon Law was *stipendium*, a word no longer used in Roman documents. According to canon 946, mass offerings are a contribution "to the good of the church . . . for the support of its ministers and works." A priest may accept only one such offering per day, no matter how many Masses he may celebrate. The medieval theology that stated that a priest could direct "special fruits" of a Mass because of accepting a "stipend" has not been repeated in official documents on mass stipends or offerings since 1974, and was criticized as being suggestive of simony.

OFFERTORY (1) – In the Tridentine Missal, *offertory* was the title given to the **preparation of the gifts**. That name is now seen to be theologically misleading, since no real offering takes place while the elements are being prepared and placed on the altar. Thus the title *offertory* is no longer used in the revised Missal. The real **offering** takes place through the *sacrifice of praise* proclaimed through the **eucharistic prayer**.

OIL OF THE CATECHUMENS (2) – Also called "Holy Oil." It is an oil specially blessed by a bishop at the **chrism Mass** and used during the initiation process of unbaptized adults and at the baptism of infants. It is stored in vials (**stocks**) labeled *O.C.* or *O.S.* (for *Oleum Sanctum*).

OIL OF THE SICK (2) – An oil specially blessed by a bishop at the **chrism Mass** and used in celebrating the **anointing of the sick**. It is stored in vials (**stocks**) labeled *O.I.* (for *Oleum Infirmorum*).

OMBRELLINO (3) – A large umbrella, with a specially bent stem, that could be carried by a minister over a priest carrying the **blessed sacrament**.

OMOPHORION (3) – The pallium-like vestment worn by all **bishops** of the **Byzantine Rite** over their outer vestment. It is worn wrapped around the neck, with one end hanging down the front and the other down the back, and overlapping on the left shoulder. The Roman **pallium** is basically a miniature version of the *omophorion*.

OPENING PRAYER (2) – Another name for the **collect**.

ORANS (2) – A posture of prayer in which the arms are uplifted toward heaven, stretched out slightly forward. Many old icons depict the saints in prayer with arms in this position. It is the position used by the presiding priest when saying public **presidential prayers** at liturgies. While saying private prayers, the priest keeps his hands joined. In the Tridentine Missal, certain public prayers of blessing were also said with hands joined, rather than extended in the *orans* position. In some parts of the world the people also use the *orans* posture (e.g. the present practice in Italy during the Lord's Prayer).

ORARION (3) – The deacon's **stole** as worn in the **Byzantine Rite**. It is worn either hanging over the left shoulder with the front end always held by the right hand, or, in some countries, worn over the left shoulder, wrapped under the right arm and draped over the left shoulder again.

ORDINARY OF THE MASS (2) – Those mass texts that do not vary (but may not always be used at every Mass, such as the **Gloria** and the **Creed**). The *ordinary* of the Mass is often contrasted with the **proper** of the Mass, which contains those texts that are special to the **feast** being celebrated. (GIRM 41)

ORDINARY TIME (1) – The two sections of the church year between the end of the Christmas season (on the Feast of the Baptism of Christ) and the beginning of Lent (on Ash Wednesday), and between the end of the Easter season (on Pentecost Sunday) and the beginning of Advent. It can be considered as a general *liturgical season* unrelated to any feast. (GIRM 316c, 323)

ORDINATION (2) – The rite of conferring the sacrament of **holy orders** on someone, either to the order of **deacon**, or **presbyter (priest)**, or **bishop**. The term formerly was also used when speaking about conferring one of the **minor orders** on someone, but now the rites speak about the **institution** of a minor minister.

ORDO (2) – A term used for the *order* or **ordinary** of the Mass, especially used of the Roman *ordines* that described the early Roman liturgies. *Ordo* or *order* is also used interchangeably with **rite** to designate other services as well, as in the *Order of Christian Funerals*. The term is also used for the booklet containing the annual calendar that indicates which feasts occur on which days, and which texts are to be used in the celebration of Mass and of the liturgy of the hours on a specific day.

ORTHODOXY (3) – Derived from the Greek word for *correct praise* (i.e., right worship), and also meaning *correct belief*. *Orthodoxy* can imply the same ideas as *lex orandi, lex credendi*. The title *Orthodox* is used by Eastern Christians who are in communion with the Patriarch of Constantinople after the Great Schism of **1054**, and is frequently applied to the **Byzantine Rite** and its style of worship.

ORTHOPRAXIS (3) – Derived from the Greek word for *correct actions* and frequently used in conjunction with **orthodoxy**. The implication is that correct worship of God leads to correct interaction with other people.

OSTENSORIUM (3) – Another name for the **monstrance**.

OTTO, RUDOLF (1869–1937) (3) – Theologian who specialized in the history and phenomenology of religion. Author of *The Idea of the Holy*.

PALL, CHALICE (2) – A flat, square, cloth covered board, about six inches on a side, that is used to cover the chalice to keep insects out. Its use at Mass was required by the Tridentine Missal, but now it is optional. (GIRM 80b, 103)

PALL, FUNERAL (2) – The white cloth used to cover the coffin of the deceased during the funeral Mass. It is a reminder of the baptismal garment.

PALLIUM (2) – The special vestment worn by archbishops. It is a two inch wide circular band made of white woolen cloth with black crosses embroidered on it. It is worn encircling the neck, over the shoulders. Byzantine Rite bishops wear a similar vestment called the **omophorion**.

PALM SUNDAY – See Passion [Palm] Sunday.

PALMS (2) – Branches waved during the Lord's entry into Jerusalem at Passover time before his death. Palms or branches of other trees are blessed on **Passion [Palm] Sunday**, as part of an elongated entrance procession. Leftover palms are burned and used as **ashes** on Ash Wednesday the next Lent.

PANNICULUS (3) – A Latin word for a *small cloth*. It is the word used in the old Pontifical to describe the linen cloth used to bind the hands of a newly-ordained priest after they were anointed during his ordination. The hands were kept bound while the newly-ordained was handed the chalice and paten with host. This cloth was often given to the priest's family, and sometimes was wrapped around the hands of the priest's mother after her death, so that she would be buried with it. It was occasionally called the *manutergium* (a generic Latin word for hand-towel and frequently used to refer to the **finger towel**) or the *mappula* (a word meaning *napkin*).

PARALITURGY (2) – The name sometimes given to a religious gathering or service that is not found in any official liturgical book. A common example is a "holy hour" that includes hymns, prayers and sermons.

PARSCH, PIUS (1884–1956) (3) – German liturgist and author of *Year of Grace* (among other works). He is noted for his efforts in the popular catechesis on the liturgy.

PASCHA (2) – The Greek word which translates the Hebrew word for **Passover**. It is also used for Christ's own "pass-over" from death to life (Jn 13:1), that is, for the Resurrection, or Easter. Many Eastern Christians prefer the term *Pascha* to **Easter** when referring to Christ's resurrection. *Pascha*, when referring to Christ and Christians, may have two meanings: *passage*, reminiscent of the passage through the Red Sea of the Hebrews fleeing Egypt after the first Passover, and the passage of Christ through death to life; and *passion*, in the sense of suffering, especially of Christ himself. The first meaning tends to emphasize the *community*, and the second (and possibly older) meaning tends to emphasize *Christ*. Thus the first meaning tends to emphasize the mystery into which every Christian of every age grows, and the second meaning emphasizes the historical events which occurred when Christ died. Both meanings are intertwined in the liturgical texts.

PASCHAL CANDLE (2) – Alternate name for the **Easter Candle**.

PASCHAL MYSTERY (2) – The title given to the mystery of Christ's death and resurrection. In general, it refers to any event in which the experience of joy through sorrow, or life through death is achieved in union with Christ's own experience during the period from **Good Friday** through **Easter** Sunday. Dom **Prosper Guéranger** was the first modern author to use the term in his writings.

PASSION [PALM] SUNDAY (2) – The Sunday before Easter, and the day which begins **Holy Week**. On this day, the entry of Christ into Jerusalem before his death is commemorated. During this entry, the gospels record that people waved branches and shouted "Hosanna." During Masses on this day, palms or other branches are blessed as part of the introductory rites, and the account of the Lord's passion is read as the gospel passage.

PASSIONTIDE (3) – A name formerly used for the last two weeks of Lent. The Fifth Sunday of Lent was formerly called the first Sunday in *Passiontide*, and on that Sunday all statues and crosses in churches were covered with purple veils. These veils were removed during the *Gloria* of the **Easter Vigil**. The revised Missal allows the veiling but does not require it, and has dropped the special terminology for this two week period.

PASSOVER (2) – The Jewish feast commemorating the Exodus from Egypt (Ex 12). Jesus celebrated the Last Supper and died in the context of the Passover feast (cf. Jn 12:1) and his **paschal mystery** is sometimes called his *passover*. Paul (1 Cor 5:7) refers to Christ himself as our *passover*. The word is translated into Greek as **Pascha**.

PATEN (1) – The older name for the **plate** on which the eucharistic bread is placed.

PAUL VI (1897–1978) (3) – Born Giovanni Montini and elected pope in 1963. He continued the Second Vatican Council convened by **Pope John XXIII**, and promulgated its documents. He also approved and promulgated all the liturgical rites revised at the mandate of the council.

PEACE, SIGN (KISS) OF – See **Sign of Peace**.

PENANCE (1) – The official title for the sacrament during which a penitent confesses sins and receives **absolution**. It is commonly called **confession** or **reconciliation**.

PENITENTIAL RITE (1) – The short ritual expression of sinfulness that normally takes place as part of the **introductory rites** of the Mass. It follows the initial greeting and precedes the *Gloria* (if prescribed) and opening prayer. Even though a "confession of sins" before offering the eucharist is mentioned in the **Didache** (ch. 14), the public and communal penitential rite in the revised Missal is a novelty, since in the Tridentine Mass the expression of sinfulness was a private action between the presiding priest and his ministers. The present rite has several formats, one being a modified version of the former confession of sin (or **Confíteor**) from the Tridentine Missal, and another using the **Kyrie** with invocations to Christ. When another liturgical action is joined to the beginning of Mass (e.g. reception of infants for baptism, blessing of candles on February 2, blessing of palms on Passion [Palm] Sunday, reception of the coffin at funeral Masses, celebration of the psalms of morning prayer or evening prayer), the *penitential rite* is omitted. It is omitted on Ash Wednesday also, since the blessing and imposition of ashes after the homily itself is a penitential rite. It is also omitted whenever the rite of blessing and sprinkling water (formerly called the **Asperges**) takes place at Sunday Masses.

PENTECOST (1) – The fiftieth and final day of the **Easter** season. It is the eighth Sunday of the Easter season (counting Easter as the first Sunday). In particular, it commemorates the descent of the Holy Spirit on the disciples as narrated in Acts 2:1–12. The celebration of Easter concludes with evening prayer on *Pentecost* and **Ordinary Time** resumes on the next day.

PEW (1) – The standard name given to the long benches on which the assembly may sit during liturgies.

PHELON(ION) (3) – The external garment of priests in the Byzantine Rite. It is similar to a **chasuble**, but it only comes down to the waist in front and functions both as a **chasuble** and a **cope**.

PHOS HILARON (3) – The major song of praise sung during **evening prayer** in the **Byzantine Rite**. It is a praise of God as the light of the world, and usually is sung immediately after the Entrance of Vespers. It is usually translated as "O Gladsome Light."

PLANNER (2) – Someone who helps prepare for a liturgical celebration by choosing hymns, readings, prayer texts, and otherwise planning the celebration. Some liturgists suggest that a more fitting term would be **preparer**. (cf. GIRM 313)

PLATE (2) – The dish on which eucharistic bread is placed during the celebration of the eucharist. The older term was **paten**. Normally, there should be only one large plate that contains all the eucharistic bread, rather than reserving one vessel for the bread eaten by the priest, and a different vessel for the bread distributed to the assembly. (GIRM 289, 292, 293)

PONTIFICAL (2) – The book that contains rites normally celebrated by a bishop, such as **confirmation**, **ordination**, and the **dedication of churches**. In the plural (*pontificals*), it refers to the distinctive accessories normally worn or used by a bishop, such as the **pectoral cross**, the **ring**, the **miter**, or the **crosier**.

PORTER (3) – One of the **minor orders** that was abolished in 1972. The duty of the *porter* was to open and close the church doors.

PRAYER AFTER COMMUNION (2) – One of the **presidential prayers**. It is said after the distribution of communion and any subsequent hymn of praise, and concludes the **liturgy of the eucharist**. After this prayer, the announcements and the **concluding rite** follow. (GIRM 10, 56k)

PRAYER OVER THE GIFTS (2) – One of the **presidential prayers**. It is said at the conclusion of the **preparation of the gifts** and it immediately precedes the **eucharistic prayer**. It was formerly called the **secret**. (GIRM 10, 53)

PRAYER OVER THE PEOPLE (2) – A prayer of blessing, addressed to God, that may immediately precede the standard formula of blessing. In the Tridentine Missal, the *prayer over the people* was only found in Lenten weekday Mass formularies. Now its use is at the discretion of the presider. (GIRM 57a)

PRAYERS (PRESIDENTIAL) (1) – The prayers that the presiding priest prays audibly in the name of the entire assembly. In particular, they are the **eucharistic prayer** (first and foremost), the opening prayer (also called the **collect**), the prayer concluding the **general intercessions**, the **prayer over the gifts**, and the **prayer after communion**. (GIRM 10, 12)

PRAYERS AT THE FOOT OF THE ALTAR (3) – The name given to the introductory rites of the Tridentine Mass. They consisted of an alternating recitation of part of Psalm 43 and a double recitation of the **Confíteor** while standing on the sanctuary floor, at the *foot* of the altar steps. Originally a private preparation of the priest and his assistants recited during the procession to the sanctuary, the prayers were recited inaudibly and were never considered a public part of the liturgy. These prayers were transformed into the public **penitential rite** during the revision of the Mass.

PRAYERS OF THE FAITHFUL (2) – An earlier name for the **general intercessions**. (GIRM 45)

PREACHING (2) – The act of giving a formal religious speech. Preaching done during a liturgical service by ordained ministers that is formally related to the feast or the readings is called a **homily**.

PRECES (3) – Intercessory prayers, often in the form of a litany. In the **liturgy of the hours**, the intercessions ending **morning prayer** and **evening prayer** are frequently called *preces*. Before the revision of the divine office, *preces* were said only on Wednesdays and Fridays during penitential times (e.g. Lent, Advent, ember days).

PRECONIUM (3) – An alternate name for the **Exsúltet**.

PREDELLA (2) – The platform or step on which an altar is set in many churches, and on which the priest stands when at the altar.

PREFACE (2) – The first section of the **eucharistic prayer**, starting with the dialogue and ending with the **Sanctus**. The name is derived from a Latin word for *proclamation*, rather than meaning something that comes *before* something else. In the present Missal, only the **Exsúltet** is in the style of a *preface*, but in the Tridentine Missal, there were several blessings in a similar style, even including the introductory dialogue (e.g. blessing of baptismal water, blessing of palms). (GIRM 55a, 108)

PREPARATION OF THE ALTAR AND GIFTS (2)—The first section of the **liturgy of the eucharist**, during which the bread and wine are placed on the **altar**. This section ritualizes the TAKING of bread and wine by Jesus, and concludes with the **prayer over the gifts**. The Tridentine

Missal called this section the **offertory**, a title now seen to be liturgically incorrect. (GIRM 48-9)

PREPARER (3) – An alternate name for a **planner**. Some contemporary liturgists suggest that *preparer* is a better and more accurate term, based on the biblical model of preparing for the Last Supper by Peter and John (cf. Lk 22:8-13).

PRE-SANCTIFIED, MASS (LITURGY) OF THE – See **Mass of the Pre-Sanctified.**

PRESBYTER (2) – A term derived from the Greek word for *elder*. It describes the second rank in the sacrament of **holy orders**, but commonly the word **priest** is used in its place. (GIRM 60)

PRESBYTERIANISM (3) – The Presbyterian form of worship is derived from John Knox's book of prayers which became the first *Book of Common Order* in 1564. It provided no fixed liturgy, but gave some prayers that the minister could use if he wished. The eucharist was celebrated infrequently, and eventually the entire calendar was abandoned. More traditional practices have been re-introduced in recent reforms.

PRESBYTERIUM (2) – The area where **presbyters** normally exercise their ministry in a church building. It includes the area around the altar and the area where the presidential **chair** and seats for concelebrants are located. In common use, *presbyterium* and **sanctuary** are interchangeable, although technically the sanctuary includes the *presbyterium*, the **ambo** and, in some churches, places for the **cantor** and the **choir**. (cf. GIRM 257-8)

PRESIDENTIAL CHAIR – See Chair, Presidential.

PRESIDER (2) – The title frequently given to the *presiding priest*. Its first use seems to be by **Justin Martyr**, and it emphasizes the functional role of presidency, rather than the static rank of **priest**. It also differs from the term **celebrant**, in that, even though every one in the assembly may *celebrate* including **concelebrating priests**, only one person in the assembly can *preside* over it all. Formerly, when a bishop was present at a Mass celebrated by a priest, the bishop was said to *preside*, even though he did not function liturgically in any capacity. (cf. GIRM 59; LM 38-42)

PRIE-DIEU (2) – Alternate name for a **kneeler**.

PRIEST (1) – The title usually given (in English) to the second rank of minister, one who has received the sacrament of **holy orders** and who, by reason of that **ordination**, is normally authorized to preside at a Mass. It is a common alternative to the title **presbyter**. Technically, there is only one *priest*, Jesus Christ (Heb 2:18, 4:14), and both *presbyters* and *bishops* share in Christ's priesthood when they preside at the altar. Thus, when the official liturgical texts speak about "priests," they frequently mean both *presbyters* and *bishops*. *Priest* is a translation of the Latin *sacerdos* and Greek *hiereus*, while *presbyter* is itself a Latin word, a close transliteration of the Greek *presbuteros*, meaning *elder*. Another use of the term *priest* is more general, since all Christians, by their baptism, can be said to form a "royal priesthood" (1 Pet 2:9), the priesthood of the **laity**. (GIRM 7)

PRIME (3) – One of the **canonical hours**, now suppressed, formerly prayed in the early morning between morning prayer (*lauds*) and mid-morning prayer (*terce*).

PROCESSION (1) – Any formal movement of several people from one place to another. For greatest solemnity, a procession is led by a thurifer, who is immediately followed by a cross-bearer between two ministers with candles. A typical Mass may include several processions: at the entrance, the gospel, the preparation of the gifts, communion, and following the dismissal. (GIRM 25, 50, 303)

PROCESSION WITH THE GIFTS (2) – The procession that takes place at the beginning of the **liturgy of the eucharist** in which members of the assembly bring forward the bread and wine for the eucharist and the monetary offerings for the church and the poor. (GIRM 49, 101)

PROFESSION OF FAITH (2) – The formula that states what the individual or community believes in as Christians. At Mass, if required, it occurs after the **homily** and usually takes one of three forms: the narrative **Nicene Creed** (prescribed on Sundays and **solemnities**); the shorter, narrative **Apostles' Creed** (allowed at Masses with children and in certain countries by decree of the conference of bishops); or the question and answer form based on the Apostles' Creed (at Masses in which infants are baptized and at the Easter Vigil). (GIRM 43)

PROFESSION, RELIGIOUS (2) – The rite of taking vows by members of religious institutes. The Missal provides mass formularies for these occasions, and the actual rite is found in the revised **Roman Ritual** or in the special rituals of the various religious institutes.

PROGRESSIVE SOLEMNITY (3) – The principle that guides the choice of what should be sung, depending on the rank of the feast, the size and composition of the assembly, the availability of music ministers and other ministers, etc. (General Instruction of the Liturgy of the Hours, 273)

PROPER OF THE MASS (2) – The texts that change from day to day. The complete *proper* for major feasts includes the antiphons for the entrance and communion, the readings, the presidential prayers, and the preface. (GIRM 41, 323)

PROSPHORA (3) – The loaf of leavened **bread** used for the eucharist in the **Byzantine Rite**.

PROTHESIS (3) – The side table or altar at which the rite of preparation takes place in the **Byzantine Rite**. This rite of preparation occurs prior to the audible part of the liturgy, and sometimes is given the name *prothesis* as well.

PSALM (2) – A selection from the book of psalms in the Old Testament. Psalms are frequently sung in the liturgy while processions take place or while certain repeated actions are performed (as at ordinations). A **responsorial psalm** is sung after the first reading during the **liturgy of the word**. (GIRM 36)

PULPIT (2) – An alternate name for an **ambo** or **lectern**. In many older churches, there was a special *pulpit* for preaching in the midst of the assembly, which was not used in the liturgy for the proclamation of scriptural readings.

PURIFICATION (2) – The cleansing of those vessels that held the eucharistic elements. This cleansing may take place after communion or after Mass and may be done by the deacon or another appropriate minister. Formerly, this was called the **ablutions**. (GIRM 120, 237–8)

PURIFICATOR (2) – The napkin-like cloth used to wipe the edge of the **cup** containing the wine for the eucharist, and normally used to dry the cup after its cleansing (i.e., **purification**). Formerly, the *purificator* was always white with a red cross sewn in its center. It was also always rectangular in shape, folded length-wise in thirds and then folded in half, so that the red cross would be visible on the fold. Because of its contact with the consecrated elements, purificators could only be washed by priests or individuals approved by the local bishop. The shape and location of the embroidered cross distinguished the purificator from the corporal and the finger towel. These restrictions no longer exist. In the Byzantine Rite, the purificator is normally red. (GIRM 80c, 244)

PYX (2) – A container for the eucharistic bread, specifically, the small containers used to carry communion to the sick. (GIRM 292)

QUINCEANERA (3) – A religious presentation ceremony celebrated around a woman's fifteenth birthday. It is a custom of Mexican origin, and as presently celebrated in the southwest United States, consists of a Mass with a renewal of baptismal vows.

QUINQUAGESIMA SUNDAY (3) – *The Fiftieth [Day] Sunday*—The Sunday before Ash Wednesday (approximately the fiftieth day before Easter), and the last Sunday in the pre-Lenten season in the calendar of the Tridentine Missal. (See entries for **Septuagesima** and **Sexagesima** Sundays.)

R.C.I.A. (2) – The standard abbreviation for the **Rite of Christian Initiation of Adults**.

READER (1) – The person who proclaims the readings before the gospel during the **liturgy of the word**, also called a **lector**. The *reader's* office conveys the truth that "in the liturgy God is speaking to his people and Christ is still proclaiming his Gospel" (**Constitution on the Sacred Liturgy** 33). The reader proclaims the appointed reading at the **ambo** and there should be a different reader for each biblical reading. Readers may be blessed or commissioned for their ministry by a special rite of **institution**. Formerly, it was regarded as one of the **minor orders**. (GIRM 66, 148–152; LM 49, 51–52)

RECONCILIATION (2) – The name given to any action of healing relationships wounded in some way. It is commonly used as an alternate title for **confession** or the sacrament of **penance**. It is used in liturgical texts (e.g. the Eucharistic Prayers for Reconciliation) to indicate the re-establishment of a good relationship between God and the human race through the life and death of Jesus.

RECONCILIATION ROOM (CHAPEL) (2) – The common name for the place where the sacrament of **penance** is celebrated according to the revised rite. This name distinguishes this place from a **confessional** which usually did not permit the celebration of the sacrament face-to-face.

REENACTMENT (3) – A repetition of some event with the implication that the original importance is not duplicated. The eucharist is sometimes termed a *reenactment* of the Last Supper.

REFORMATION (3) – The period of historical events in the sixteenth century that led to divisions in western Christianity and the establishment of independent Protestant Churches. One of the major leaders was **Martin Luther** in Germany.

REFORMED LITURGY (3) – The style of worship that finds its origin in the reformation and the reformed churches. It emphasizes the proclamation of the word of God and preaching, and de-emphasizes sacraments, symbols, and rituals.

RELICS, SAINTS' (2) – Particles of bone or something else related to a saint. The Tridentine Missal required the presence of relics of martyrs within the altar or in a smaller **altar stone**, but the presence of relics is now optional. It is preferred that relics be large enough to be recognizable as parts of human bodies, and that they be placed under the altar, rather than into a niche carved into the altar top. (GIRM 266)

RELIQUARY (3) – Any container for **relics**. Frequently *reliquaries* are designed to look like small **monstrances**.

REPOSE, ALTAR OF (2) – The place and **tabernacle** used on **Holy Thursday** evening to reserve the eucharistic bread to be used at the **Good Friday** service. It should be appropriately decorated before midnight, but very subdued on Good Friday itself. The title *altar of repose* is derived from the Tridentine Missal, but in the revised Missal the place need no longer be an "altar," and need not be distinct from the usual tabernacle of reservation, if it is already in a reservation **chapel** separated from the main body of the church.

REQUIEM MASS (3) – A generic name for a Mass of the dead. The name is frequently applied to the musical compositions written for the texts sung by the assembly or choir, especially for the texts found in the Tridentine Missal, e.g. *Verdi's Requiem.* (cf. GIRM 335 ff.)

REREDOS (3) – The artistic backwall behind the high altar, especially if the altar were attached to a wall, as was customary before 1964. Such a backwall frequently had paintings and statues built into it.

RES TANTUM (3) – *The reality ("thing") alone*—A standard category used in sacramental theology to describe the *grace* of a sacrament, that which is signified and caused through the visible ritual action and the texts. (See the entries on **sacramentum et res** and **sacramentum tantum** below.)

RESERVATION, EUCHARISTIC (2) – The practice of keeping some of the consecrated elements in a **tabernacle** to be used for viaticum for the dying, and also as a focus for prayer and worship. (GIRM 276–7)

RESPONSES (1) – The answers made by the assembly to the various prayers and greetings given by the priest, deacon or other minister during the celebration of Mass. (GIRM 15, 36, 90)

RESPONSORIAL PSALM (1) – The **psalm** used as a response to the **first reading**, also called the **gradual**. It is normally proclaimed responsorially, with a psalmist singing the text of the psalm and the assembly responding with a response antiphon. (GIRM 36; LM 19–22)

RESPONSORY (3) – The scriptural verses, usually taken from the psalms, used as a response to the scriptural reading during the celebration of one of the **canonical hours**. The method of executing the *responsory* differs from the method in which the responsorial psalm during Mass is executed.

RING, BISHOP'S (2) – A ring, frequently with a jewel, worn by a Roman Rite bishop on the ring finger of his right hand. It is given to the bishop at his episcopal ordination, and symbolizes the marriage to the diocese.

RING, WEDDING (2) – The ring or rings blessed and given at the celebration of **marriage**. The rite presupposes that a ring will always be given by the husband to his wife, but the giving of a ring by the wife to her husband is optional.

RIPIDION (3) – A liturgical fan, usually mounted on a pole and carried in processions, commonly used in the **Byzantine Rite**. The fan is usually circular, depicting the face of a seraph with six wings, and often having tiny bells.

RITE (2) – The title of any official liturgical ceremony, such as the **Rite of Christian Initiation of Adults**. It is sometimes interchangeable with *order* or *ordo*, as in the *Order of Mass*, or used to describe a section of a larger ceremony, such as the **concluding rite** of the Mass. (GIRM 57) *Rite* also refers to a ritual family usually associated with a particular territory, which includes the individual traditions, feasts, canon law, ways of celebrating the eucharist and the sacraments, and including an approach to theology as well. The two major rites in the Catholic Church are the **Roman Rite** and the **Byzantine Rite** (also used by Orthodox Christians). (cf. LM 59; canons 111, 214)

RITE OF CHRISTIAN INITIATION OF ADULTS (2) – The collection of ceremonies by which a person celebrates his or her incorporation into the Catholic Church. The rite begins with admission into the **catechumenate**, reaches a high point with **baptism**, **confirmation**, and **communion** at the **Easter Vigil**, and concludes with a period of **mystagogy**. It is standardly abbreviated as **R.C.I.A.**

RITUAL (1) – A name given to any formalized action. Normally, it refers to special religious activities that have a set structure and order, and employs religious symbols and texts. In general, however, *ritual* is any human activity that occurs when people creatively give life to expected patterns of behavior or rules of action. Examples of secular rituals include folk dancing, sports games and customs (e.g. the seventh inning stretch), and birthday traditions. Both secular and religious rituals include rules (or **rubrics**), repeated behavior by key "celebrants," and expectations by the "assembly." Good ritual also involves an aspect of creativity and ingenuity within the familiar framework.

RITUAL, ROMAN (3) – The general title for the books which contain the prayers and rites for the celebrations of the sacraments and blessings. In general, the *Ritual* contains all rites except for the Mass (found in the **Roman Missal**), the **liturgy of the hours**, and those used by a bishop (found in the **Pontifical**). The old *Ritual* used to contain all prayers in one book, but the revision of the rites has necessitated separate books for each of the sacraments, for services like funerals or religious profession, and for the various blessings (contained in the 1984 **Book of Blessings**).

ROGATION DAYS (3) – The three days of special prayer and intercession in the calendar of the Tridentine Missal that came before Ascension Thursday.

ROMAN MISSAL – See **Missal, Roman**.

ROMAN RITE (3) – The ritual system used by the Pope of Rome and those associated with that tradition. It is noted for its starkness, simplicity, practicality, sobriety and dignity. It is in marked contrast with other Rites in the Catholic Church, such as the **Byzantine Rite**, whose ceremonies are marked by the use of much symbolism and repetition. (LM 59, 62)

ROMAN RITUAL – See **Ritual, Roman**.

ROOD SCREEN (3) – A screen or wall that separated the **choir** section of a church from the **nave** in some medieval-style churches. Doorways corresponding to the aisles in the church existed to allow passage between the choir and the nave. Frequently the screen was surmounted by a cross (*rood*) over the center passageway.

ROSARY (2) – A devotion consisting of prescribed set of prayers said while meditating on events (usually called *mysteries*) related to the lives of Christ or his mother. Usually the prayers are counted by means of a set of prayer beads, also called a *rosary* or *crown*. The common form of the rosary consists of a set of 54 beads on a circular string attached to single string of five beads and a crucifix. The 54 beads are arranged into five groups of ten beads each (called *decades*), each separated by a space and a larger bead. Each decade corresponds to a prescribed mystery. While meditating on each of the mysteries, the **Hail Mary** is said ten times using the ten beads to keep count. Each decade is preceded by the recitation of the Lord's Prayer and followed by the Glory to the Father. It was formerly common for Catholics to say the rosary one or more times while attending a Mass which was said in Latin. It was also common for priests to have the obligation to recite the **divine office** commuted to the recitation of the rosary one or more times.

RUBRIC (2) – A direction or explanatory instruction printed between prayers or other texts of a liturgical rite. The word *rubric* is derived from the Latin word for *red*, since the rubrics are normally printed in red in the liturgical books. Some rubrics are descriptive (and thus may be adapted in certain situations), and others are prescriptive (absolutely prescribing what must be done). Unfortunately, in many cases, it is difficult to distinguish the importance of a rubric from its wording.

Rubrics are meant to give structure and order to a **ritual** similar to the way that regulations give structure and order to secular gatherings.

SABBATH (2) – The seventh day of the week, the day on which God rested after creation (Gen 2:2). In English, it is usually called Saturday. One of the Ten Commandments forbids work on the Sabbath (Ex 20:8–11) and commands praise of God. The Christians changed their day of worship to Sunday, the day on which Christ rose from the dead.

SACRAMENT (1) – In the most general definition, it is a *visible sign of invisible divine grace*. Thus, the ultimate basic sacrament is Christ—a visible sign of God's presence on this earth. Next is the Church, which, according to the Dogmatic Constitution on the Church of the Second Vatican Council, "is like the sacrament or sign and instrument of intimate union with God" (n. 1). Most commonly, *sacrament* refers to one of seven specially designated ritual activities. They are: **baptism, confirmation, eucharist, penance, matrimony, holy orders, anointing of the sick**. Each of these *sacraments* is frequently described by reference to a key material action or object **(matter)** that is joined to a prayer-filled liturgical text **(form)**. The eucharist is often called the **blessed sacrament**. (GIRM 56i)

SACRAMENTAL (2) – "A sacred sign by which spiritual effects especially are signified and are obtained by the intercession of the Church" (canon 1166). Among the common actions and objects considered *sacramentals* are blessed medals, **blessings**, **palms**, **holy water**, the **rosary**. (GIRM 326)

SACRAMENTARY (2) – The book of prayers used by the presiding priest during the celebration of the Mass. It is part of the **Roman Missal**, and is complementary to the **lectionary**. (Introduction to GIRM 8)

SACRAMENTUM ET RES (3) – *The symbol and the reality ("thing")*—A category used in sacramental theology to describe the symbolic reality (normally visible). It refers to the permanent element effected, that which holds permanently the significance of the rite and continues to signify the grace. In the eucharist, the consecrated elements are the *sacramentum et res*. (See the entries for **res tantum** and **sacramentum tantum**.)

SACRAMENTUM TANTUM (3) – *The symbol alone*—A category used in sacramental theology to describe the visible rite of a sacrament, that is the words and actions that make up the sacramental experience. (See the entries for **res tantum** and **sacramentum et res**.)

SACRARIUM (2) – The special sink, usually with an attached cover, whose drain goes directly into an earthen pit rather than to a sewer. Water used for cleansing vessels used at the eucharist (and similar items) is poured into the sacrarium. (GIRM 239)

SACRED HEART, SOLEMNITY OF THE (2) – A feast of Christ celebrated on the second Friday after Pentecost. Devotion to the Sacred Heart has also led the custom of celebrating votive Masses of the Sacred Heart on the **first Friday** of each month.

SACRIFICE (1) – A means by which communication is established with and reverence is offered to God by a human being. In the Hebrew Scriptures, *sacrifice* is frequently associated with the destruction of a victim, such as the burnt offering sacrifices of Cain and Abel, or the attempted sacrifice of Isaac by Abraham. However, even in the psalms, praise and thanksgiving are considered to be sacrifices (Ps 50:23, 116:17), and love and mercy are considered more important than sacrifices and holocausts (Hos 6:6). The Mass is considered a sacrifice in that it makes present the ultimate sacrifice of Jesus on the cross (Heb 7:27, 9:12), but it is also a bloodless "sacrifice of praise" (Sir 35:1-2) offered through the prayers, hymns, and lives of the assembly. (GIRM 7, 54, 55d)

SACRISTY (2) – The room that stores vestments and liturgical items used in a church, and is used for preparation. It is also commonly used as a vesting room, although larger churches and cathedrals may have a separate vesting room, called the **secretarium**. (GIRM 81)

SACROSANCTUM CONCILIUM (3) – The Latin title of the **Constitution on the Sacred Liturgy** of the Second Vatican Council.

SAINTS (2) – Women and men of ages past who are noted for their holiness of life and heroic virtue, and are honored in the liturgy and the calendar. Presently, before someone can be publicly called a *saint*, there is a formal investigation into a person's background and a formal rite of canonization by the pope.

SALT (2) – *Salt* was formerly required in blessing **holy water**. The present Missal permits its use when water is blessed and sprinkled as part of the introductory rites, but does not require it. Salt was also formerly used in the rite of baptism, but has been dropped in the revision of the rite.

SANCTORALE (2) – The section of the Missal that contains the texts for saints' feasts.

SANCTUARY (1) – The area of a church in which the **presidential chair**, **altar**, and **ambo** are located, and in which the major ministers also may sit. Normally it is elevated for the sake of visibility. Formerly, the area was separated from the place for the assembly by a **communion rail**. It is sometimes also called the **presbyterium** or **chancel**. (GIRM 258)

SANCTUARY LIGHT (CANDLE / LAMP) (2) – The candle required to be kept burning near the tabernacle when the sacrament is reserved (canon 940). According to the 1973 section of the revised **Roman Ritual** on *Holy Communion and Worship of the Eucharist outside of Mass* (n. 11), this lamp is to be either of oil or of wax.

SANCTUS (2) – The hymn sung as an initial acclamation during the **eucharistic prayer**, which thus marks the end of the **preface** section of the prayer. It employs the hymn of the angels as recorded in Isaiah 6:3 and Revelation 4:8. In English, it is often called the **Holy, Holy, Holy**.

SARAPION – See Serapion.

SCHMEMANN, ALEXANDER (1921–1983) (3) – Orthodox liturgical theologian and author of numerous books. He attempted to synthesize the older style of allegorical reflection on the Byzantine liturgical rites, with both a modern historical appreciation of the origin of these rites and contemporary theological reflection.

SCRUTINY (2) – A rite of prayer and self-examination celebrated on the Third, Fourth and Fifth Sundays of Lent for the **elect**, that is, those in the **R.C.I.A.** who will be initiated at the **Easter Vigil**. The rite occurs at the end of the **liturgy of the word**, includes a prayer of **exorcism**, and concludes with the **dismissal** of the elect.

SEASON, LITURGICAL (1) – An extended period of time during the church year that is similar to a natural season of the year. There are four *seasons* that prepare for and extend the celebration of the two major feasts of the Church year: the **Advent** season prepares for Christmas and the Christmas season extends its celebration; and the season of **Lent** prepares for Easter and the Easter season extends its celebration. In addition, there is a general season between the others called **Ordinary Time**.

SECOND READING (1) – On Sundays and certain major feasts, after the **first reading** and the responsorial psalm, a *second reading* is proclaimed. It is taken from one of the books of the New Testament other than the gospels. (GIRM 91)

SECRET (3) – The former title of the **prayer over the gifts**, so-called because it was recited *silently* except for its concluding words, *per ómnia sǽcula sæculórum* ("for ever and ever").

SECRETARIUM (3) – The vesting room, distinct from the **sacristy**, from which the entrance procession begins. It is found in larger churches and cathedrals.

SEDIA GESTATORIA (3) – The portable papal throne on a platform, on which the pope sat when he was carried in procession to the altar at major papal Masses. Usually **flabella** were carried on either side of the *sedia*. The *sedia* has not been used since Pope John Paul I in 1978.

SEPTUAGESIMA SUNDAY (3) – *The Seventieth [Day] Sunday*—The third Sunday before Ash Wednesday (approximately the seventieth day before Easter), and the beginning of the pre-Lenten season in the Tridentine Missal. (See the entries for **Quinquagesima** and **Sexagesima** Sundays.)

SEQUENCE (2) – A poetic hymn that on certain feasts is sung after the **alleluia** as an additional preparation for the gospel. *Sequences* are prescribed only for Easter and Pentecost, but may also be used on the solemnity of the Body and Blood of Christ and on Our Lady of Sorrows (Sept. 15). (GIRM 40)

SERAPION (d. c. 362) (3) – Bishop of Thmuis (Nile Delta) from around 339 until his death. A *Euchologion* (collection of prayers) is attributed to him which contains many liturgical texts including a developed **eucharistic prayer**. This seems to be the earliest evidence of the inclusion of the **Sanctus** in the eucharistic prayer. The name is sometimes spelled *Sarapion*.

SERMON (1) – A generic name given to **preaching**. It can be used to describe any religious or morally oriented speech, especially if not related to any scriptural passage or any feast. The preaching done in the course of the liturgy by a bishop, priest or deacon is more properly called a **homily**.

SERVE (2) – The word used to describe assistance given to the presiding priest. The ministers who assist the presiding priest in the sanctuary are frequently called **servers**, and are said to *serve* Mass. In the Byzantine Rite, the liturgical texts speak about a priest or deacon *serving* the Divine Liturgy rather than using the western terminology of **celebrating**.

SERVER (1) – A common name given to those (especially children) who assist the presiding priest during the celebration of Mass. The official texts speak of *acolytes* and *ministers*, in addition to *servers*, but frequently the three terms are interchangeable. (GIRM 82, 209)

SERVICE (2) – A generic title used for any public worship, particularly by non-Catholics. It is often used interchangeably with **liturgy**.

SEXAGESIMA SUNDAY (3) – *The Sixtieth [Day] Sunday*— The second Sunday before Ash Wednesday (approximately the sixtieth day before Easter) in the calendar of the Tridentine Missal. (See the entries for **Quinquagesima** and **Septuagesima** Sundays.)

SICK, PASTORAL CARE OF THE (2) – The present official title of the liturgical rites pertaining to the sick and dying. It includes the sacrament of the **anointing of the sick**, the rite of **viaticum**, and the commendation of the dying.

SICK, ANOINTING OF THE – See Anointing of the Sick.

SIGN (2) – A generic name for the various objects that are used to point to a deeper reality. Often the meaning associated with a *sign* is more rational than that associated with a **symbol** and so a distinction is sometimes made between the two. Some authors suggest that *signs* perform, manipulate, and are mechanical whereas **symbols** resound, suggest, and are personal. (GIRM 240, 283)

SIGN OF PEACE (1) – The ritual greeting and exchange of words of peace during the liturgy of the eucharist, that occurs after the **Lord's Prayer** and before the **breaking of the bread**. (GIRM 56b, 136)

SILENCE (2) – The quiet reflection necessary for prayer. Moments for *silence* are highly recommended during the course of the Mass, especially during the liturgy of the word, and after communion. (GIRM 23; LM 28)

SINGING (1) – The raising of voice in musical song has always been considered a part of worship, as the ancient proverb states, "One who sings well prays twice." Jesus and the disciples sang songs of praise at the Last Supper (Mt 26:30), and this tradition has been continued in gatherings until the present day. Singing is meant to be normally done by all present, and not merely by a choir. In fact, the **alleluia** before the gospel is forbidden to be sung by a cantor or choir only. (GIRM 19, 63; LM 23)

SITTING (1) – Sitting is the posture of a teacher (cf. Jesus at the Sermon on the Mount, Mt 5:1). It is also the posture of those who listen to a teacher. The people sit at the liturgy during the readings before the gospel, during the homily, while the gifts are being prepared, and for reflection after communion. (GIRM 21)

SKULL CAP (3) – The common name for the **zucchetto**.

SOLEMN ANNUAL EXPOSITION (3) – A prolonged period of time (formerly usually lasting for forty hours over a three-day period) during which the reserved sacrament is exposed for public adoration. It was formerly called **Forty Hours Devotion**.

SOLEMN BLESSING (2) – The form of blessing in which the standard trinitarian formula is preceded by three invocations. The assembly responds to each of these invocations with "Amen." It is a standard alternative form of blessing which can be used in any Mass. (cf. GIRM 57a)

SOLEMN MASS (3) – The form of Mass celebrated according to the Tridentine Missal, in which the presiding priest was assisted by a deacon and subdeacon, at which all the prescribed texts were sung, and during which incense was always used.

SOLEMNITY (2) – The highest rank of **feast**. In the general Roman Calendar, there are only fourteen *solemnities* associated with fixed dates or in Ordinary Time (Jan 1—Mary, Mother of God; Jan 6—Epiphany; Mar 19—Joseph; Mar 25—Annunciation; June 24—Birth of the Baptist; June 29—Peter and Paul; Aug 15—Assumption; Nov 1—All Saints; Dec 8—Immaculate Conception; Dec 25—Christmas; Holy Trinity; Body and Blood of Christ; Sacred Heart; Christ the King). In addition, Easter and its preceding triduum take precedence over any solemnity of the calendar, as do the Ascension and Pentecost (which are also considered solemnities). On solemnities, both the **Gloria** and the **profession of faith** are prescribed. (GIRM 31, 44)

SOLESMES (3) – The French Benedictine abbey responsible for the renewal and codification of Gregorian chant. It was refounded in **1832** by Dom **Prosper Guéranger**.

SPACE, LITURGICAL (2) – A generic name for an area or building suitable in size and arrangement for public worship. *Liturgical space* should be arranged according to contemporary appreciation for good liturgical **architecture**. (cf. GIRM 253; EACW 39–43)

SPONSOR (2) – Someone who initially vouches for a candidate for Christian initiation or confirmation. A *sponsor* should know the candidate and be able to attest to the candidate's character, intentions and faith. The *sponsor* may be a different person from the **godparent**. (R.C.I.A. [1985 text] 10)

SPOON FOR COMMUNION (3) – A special spoon, usually gold or silver, that may be used to distribute the consecrated wine to communicants. In the Byzantine Rite, communion is always distributed using a *spoon* since the consecrated bread is placed into the chalice after the communion of the clergy. (GIRM 243b, 251)

SPOON FOR WATER (3) – A special spoon or miniature ladle that was used by some priests to get a few drops of water from the cruet to mix with the wine in the chalice during the **preparation of the gifts**. It was not very commonly used.

SPOON, INCENSE (2) – The spoon used to transfer the unburnt incense from the **boat** to the **censer**.

STANDING (1) – The standard posture of prayer. The Council of Nicaea decreed that all should stand for prayer on Sundays and during the Easter Season rather than kneel (Nicaea, canon 20). (GIRM 21)

STATIONAL MASS (3) – A Mass celebrated by the bishop of the diocese with special solemnity on major feasts and occasions. This ancient term of *station* was reintroduced in the revised **Ceremonial of Bishops**, but was mentioned in the Tridentine Missal when designating the ancient locations of papal Masses during Lent. The solemn format by which a bishop celebrates Mass was formerly called a *pontifical Mass*.

STATIONS OF THE CROSS (2) – A devotional practice that originated when the Franciscans were given custody of the Holy Land in the fourteenth century. In 1731, Pope Clement XII fixed the number at fourteen, and most churches erect paintings or sculptures of the designated biblical and traditional scenes on the inside walls of the nave. Formerly, each station had to have a wooden cross affixed to it. Some churches have added a fifteenth scene, that of the resurrection, to the traditional fourteen.

STATUES (2) – Three-dimensional images of art that provide a focal point for prayer of the assembly. Although none is required, most churches have statues of Christ or Mary and major patrons. Byzantine churches do not have statues, but have **icons** instead. (cf. GIRM 278)

STIPEND (2) – The title formerly associated with a monetary offering given to a priest for celebrating Mass for a specific intention (cf. 1917 Code of Canon Law, canon 824). The 1983 Code of Canon Law uses the title "**offering**" (*stips*) in place of "stipend" (*stipendium*) (cf. canon 945). According to Thomas Aquinas, the title "stipend" indicated that the donation was compensation for the time and labor of the priest, since the same word was formerly used to indicate the wage paid to soldiers.

STOCK, HOLY OIL (2) – A container for the holy oils of **chrism**, **oil of the sick**, and **oil of the catechumens**.

STOLE (1) – The vestment worn over the neck by ordained ministers. It is about five inches wide and on a priest or bishop it hangs down three or four feet long in front. A deacon wears a stole over his left shoulder and fastened at his waist on the right side. (GIRM 302)

STOLE FEE (2) – An offering given to a priest for performing some liturgical rite, such as a baptism, wedding, funeral, or even a Mass. In the case of a Mass, the *stole fee* is usually distinct from the Mass **offering**, since the stole fee corresponds to an honorarium given to a professional person for time and services, while the offering is given with the understanding that the priest will pray for the donor's intention. (cf. canon 848)

STOUP, HOLY WATER (2) – A container for **holy water** usually found at an entrance to a church. Their presence provides the faithful with the opportunity to bless themselves with water, a reminder of their baptism, as they enter and exit a church. The stoup is also called a **font**.

STRAW, LITURGICAL (3) – A silver tube used for receiving the consecrated wine from the chalice. A straw formerly was used by the pope at certain Masses, and its use is a permitted option in the present Missal. (cf. GIRM 243a, 248–250)

SUBDEACON (3) – Formerly, a non-sacramental major order in the Roman Rite which was suppressed by Pope Paul VI in 1972. The subdeacon wore a **tunic** at a solemn Mass and sang the epistle. In some Eastern Rites, the rank of minor clergy equivalent to the **acolyte** is called the *subdiaconate*, and the name *subdeacon* may also be used for **acolyte** in western countries as well, if the conference of bishops so decides.

SUBSTANCE (3) – The underlying reality of physical matter. It is a classical philosophical term used in distinction to **accidents**. This distinction provides the basis for the explanation of the change in the eucharistic elements in **transubstantiation**.

SUNDAY (1) – The weekly commemoration of the Lord's Resurrection. It is both the first day of the week and also the eighth day. It is also called the **Lord's Day**. (GIRM 77)

SURPLICE (2) – A white, loose tunic-like garment worn over a **cassock**. It is derived from the alb, and was formerly regularly worn by priests especially when officiating at liturgies not connected with a eucharist. In many places, **servers** at Mass vest in cassock and *surplice*. (GIRM 298)

SYMBOL (2) – A traditional name given to the **profession of faith** or **creed**. (GIRM 43)

SYMBOLS, LITURGICAL (2) – A generic name for the various traditional and contemporary designs and objects that point to something beyond themselves. *Symbol* is often distinguished from **sign**. For many, a *symbol* has a pre-conscious, historical meaning that goes much beyond the visible (e.g. water —life and death; bread—nourishment and health). A **sign** merely has a meaning agreed upon by common consent or law (e.g. a red/green traffic signal). However, this distinction is not always hard and fast. (cf. GIRM 297, 306)

SYNAXIS (3) – A gathering or **assembly** of the faithful for prayer and praise of God. The name is also applied to the service that usually occurs after such a gathering takes place, and is generally applied to any **liturgy of the word**, such as that which takes place during Mass. In the Byzantine Rite, certain feasts are given the title of *synaxis* if they have a special relation to the feast celebrated on the previous day, such as the *Synaxis* of Mary, Mother of God, celebrated on December 26.

SYNERGY (3) – A combined activity or cooperative action, such as between God, a human minister, and a human subject in the action of a sacrament.

TABERNACLE (1) – The safe-like receptacle for storing the consecrated eucharistic bread. It must always be locked while the eucharistic elements are stored in it, and a burning candle (the **sanctuary light**) should be nearby. By tradition and law, a tabernacle is the normal location to reserve the **blessed sacrament** (canons 935, 938). In medieval times, tabernacles in the shape of *doves*, sometimes suspended over the altar, were common. (GIRM 277)

TABERNACLE VEIL (2) – A veil placed over the tabernacle whenever the consecrated elements are stored within. Formerly it was called a **conopaeum**. The veil was formerly required, but the requirement was not universally observed, and in most places, the burning **sanctuary lamp** was more commonly understood as the sign of the presence of the blessed sacrament. The 1973 section of the Roman Ritual on *Holy Communion and Worship of the Eucharist outside of Mass* (n. 11) states: "The presence of the eucharist in the tabernacle is to be shown by a veil or in another suitable way determined by the competent authority."

TABLE (2) – The **altar** at which the sacred banquet of the eucharist is celebrated. Patristic texts see the **ambo** as also being a symbolic *table*, and speak about *two* tables: the table of God's word and the table of Christ's body. (GIRM 8, 259)

TE DEUM (3) – A hymn that begins with the words, *You are God, we praise you* . . . . It occurs during the *liturgy of the hours* at the end of the office of readings on Sundays when the Gloria is prescribed at Mass. It is also sung at the end of the Mass of the ordination of a bishop while the new bishop processes through the assembly to give his blessing. A *Te Deum* is also the name given to a service of thanksgiving in which the hymn is sung, such as is traditionally celebrated in some places annually on December 31.

TEMPORALE (2) – The section of the Missal that deals with the celebrations based on the **seasons** of the church year (focused on Easter and Christmas) rather than on the calendar celebrations of saints.

TENEBRAE (3) – *Matins* of Holy Thursday (now called the office of readings in the liturgy of the hours). It was formerly celebrated with great solemnity on the evening of Wednesday of **Holy Week**. During the chanting of the lessons, the candles in a seven-branched candelabrum were extinguished one by one. A high point for many was the solemn chanting of the Lamentations of Jeremiah.

THANKSGIVING (1) – The offering of gratitude and thanks to someone, particularly for some benefit received. The celebration of the Mass is termed a **eucharist** or *thanksgiving*, since Christians give thanks to a loving God for salvation and redemption accomplished through the life, death, and resurrection of Jesus Christ. The motive of thanksgiving finds expression particularly in the first part of the **eucharistic prayer**, called the *preface*. (GIRM 55a)

THEODORE OF MOPSUESTIA (c. 350–428) (3) – A fellow-student with **John Chrysostom**, he became bishop of Mopsuestia in 392. His *Catecheses* are similar to those of **Cyril of Jerusalem**, but are longer and contain more actual liturgical texts.

THEOPHANY (3) – A word derived from two Greek words: one word meaning God (*Theos*), and the other word meaning shine (*phaino*). *Theophany* refers to any manifestation of God, especially of the three persons of the Trinity together. The **Epiphany** is often called the *Theophany* in the **Byzantine Rite**, since the mystery of Christ's baptism is celebrated (rather than the visit of the Magi), at which the Trinity was manifested.

THEOTOKOS (3) – The name given by the Council of Ephesus (in the year 431) to Mary, Mother of Jesus. It means *God-bearer*, and was chosen as an alternative to *Christotokos* or *Christ-bearer*, implying that Mary gave birth to God, and not merely to a man who later was united to the divine Word. This Marian title has **Christological** implications, and is the standard title used of Mary in the **Byzantine** liturgical texts.

THRONE, BISHOP'S (2) – The older name for the **cathedra**, or bishop's special chair in the **cathedral**. Formerly, the throne was normally on the left (or gospel) side of the sanctuary and had a canopy. Now it is normally located behind the altar, so that the bishop faces the people. *Cathedra* is the preferred terminology in recent documents.

THURIBLE (2) – The older name for a **censer**. (GIRM 68)

THURIFER (2) – The older title given to the one who carried the **thurible (censer)**. (cf. GIRM 82a)

TIARA (3) – The triple crown formerly used by popes at solemn ceremonies in lieu of a **miter**. It was also called a *triregnum* or *triple-crown*, and signified the three spheres of papal authority. Its use was discontinued by Pope John Paul I in 1978.

TIME (2) – The standard measurement of change, particularly the way to delineate past and future events. The **liturgy of the hours** and the **calendar** are frequently referred to as ways to sanctify *time*.

TONSURE (3) – The rite of cutting hair from the crown or top of someone's head. Certain religious orders once practiced a rite of tonsure and kept the hair permanently shaved on the crown of the head. A liturgical rite of tonsure was formerly used to admit someone into the clerical state, and was celebrated prior to the reception of the **minor orders**. The clerical rite of tonsure was suppressed in 1972, and is replaced by a rite of *Admission to Candidacy for Ordination as Deacons and Priests*.

TRACT (2) – A hymn, usually consisting of verses of a psalm, sung before the gospel during Lent in place of the **alleluia**. In the Tridentine Missal, the *tract* immediately followed the **gradual**. In the revised Missal and lectionary, the responsorial **verse before the gospel** normally replaces the **alleluia** during Lent, but a tract taken from auxiliary books, such as the **Gradual**, may still be used. (GIRM 37b)

TRADITION (2) – The accumulated customs and wisdom, especially of the Christian community. *Tradition* is invoked in the Catholic Church with an authority that is similar (yet not equal) to that of Scripture. (GIRM 232, 282–3)

TRANSFIGURATION, FEAST OF THE (2) – The feast celebrated on August 6 that commemorates the biblical event of Christ's glory shining forth before the apostles Peter, James and John on Mount Tabor.

TRANSFINALIZATION (3) – A contemporary theological term used to explain the change of the eucharistic bread and wine into the body and blood of Christ. It attempts to base the explanation on the change in the *final purpose* or *ultimate end* of the elements for members of the community. As yet, the term has no status in official Catholic theology.

TRANSIGNIFICATION (3) – A contemporary theological term used to explain the change of the eucharistic bread and wine into the body and blood of Christ. It attempts to base the explanation on the change in the *significance* of the elements for members of the community. As yet, the term has no status in official Catholic theology.

TRANSMUTATION (3) – The word sometimes used by Orthodox Christians to explain the change of the eucharistic bread and wine into the body and blood of Christ. Orthodox Christians firmly believe in the reality of the presence of Christ's body and blood in the eucharistic elements after the **anaphora**, but some hesitate to use the western theological explanation of **transubstantiation**.

TRANSUBSTANTIATION (2) – The theological name given to the traditional Catholic explanation regarding the change of the bread and wine into the body and blood of Christ during the Eucharist. The term is based on the belief that the **substance** of the bread and wine is changed, but the external **accidents** remain unchanged. Some Orthodox Churches prefer to speak about **transmutation**, and Luther favored the term **consubstantiation**. Contemporary theologians have also used the terms **transignification** and **transfinalization**. (Introduction to GIRM 3)

TRIDENTINE MASS (2) – The common name given to the Mass celebrated according to the Missal revised by decree of the Council of Trent and promulgated in 1570. (cf. Introduction to GIRM 6)

TRIDUUM, EASTER (PASCHAL/SACRED) (2) – The three day celebration of Christ's death and resurrection. The *triduum* starts with the evening Mass of the Lord's Supper on **Holy Thursday**, reaches a high point with the celebration of the resurrection at the **Easter Vigil** and concludes with evening prayer on Easter Sunday. Contemporary authors emphasize the unity of the three days even in terms of the rites and texts of the liturgy: it is *one* worship event with three phases which are celebrated over three days. Friday's prayers speak both of death *and* resurrection. Thursday's liturgy blends into Friday's through the special reservation of the eucharist. Thursday's and Friday's liturgies never end liturgically, since they do not have blessings or dismissals—a solemn ending only occurs at the end of the Vigil. (GIRM 336; Gen. Norms for the Liturgical Year and the Calendar, 19)

TRINITY, SOLEMNITY OF THE HOLY (2) – The feast celebrated on the Sunday after Pentecost. Some national churches in the Anglican communion refer to the

Sundays between Trinity Sunday and Advent as *Sundays after Trinity*.

TRISAGION (3) – A Greek word which means *thrice-holy*. It is the title of a hymn to God's holiness, that seems to be an expansion of the initial words of the **Sanctus**. It normally is: "Holy God, Holy Mighty, Holy Immortal, have mercy on us." It is sung after the Minor Entrance at a Byzantine Liturgy, and in the Roman Rite is sung during the veneration of the cross on Good Friday.

TUNIC (3) – The outer garment formerly worn by a **subdeacon**. In style and cut it was identical to a deacon's **dalmatic**, but usually had only one cross bar as a decoration rather than the two of the **dalmatic**.

TURNER, VICTOR (1920–1983) (3) – Anthropologist who specialized in comparative religions, particularly the use of rituals and symbols. He introduced the theory of "liminality" in his book *The Ritual Process*, as a way of describing religious rites as "threshold" experiences.

USHER (1) – The common name given to someone who helps seat people as they arrive at the church for worship, who helps lead processions, and who takes up the **collection**. Sometimes they also fulfill the ministry of **greeter**. (GIRM 68b, c)

VEIL (2) – Various veils are used in the course of liturgies. The chalice has been traditionally covered with a **chalice veil** when not in use. (GIRM 80c) A priest or deacon wears a **humeral veil** when carrying the consecrated sacrament. A minister assisting a bishop may wear a light shoulder veil called a **vimpa**. During the last two weeks of Lent, the statues and crosses may be veiled in purple (formerly it was required). A veiled cross (in red) may be used for the veneration of the cross during the Good Friday liturgy. A **tabernacle veil** may be used to indicate the presence of the eucharist. Formerly, ciboria containing the eucharist had to be covered with a veil and a veil was placed before a **monstrance** when a sermon was given during an exposition of the blessed sacrament.

VERSE BEFORE THE GOSPEL (2) – The acclamation sung before the gospel during Lent that takes the place of the **alleluia**. It normally consists of a refrain addressed to Christ sung by all, and an intervening scriptural verse. (GIRM 37b, 39)

VESPERS (2) – The older name for **evening prayer**, one of the **canonical hours**.

VESTIBULE (2) – The ante-room of a church, between the front door and the **nave**. A large **vestibule** is sometimes called a **narthex**.

VESTMENTS (1) – The ritual, stylized clothing and symbols of office worn by various ministers at worship services. The common garment for ministers in the sanctuary is the **alb**, over which ordained ministers add a **stole**. Bishops and priests wear a **chasuble**, and on solemn occasions deacons may wear a **dalmatic**. (GIRM 297–310)

VIATICUM (2) – A Latin word designating *provisions for a journey*. It is the title for **communion** received before death, as nourishment for the journey to heaven. The eucharist is administered with an additional formula,

"May the Lord Jesus Christ protect you and lead you to eternal life." The complete rite also includes a final renewal of the baptismal **profession of faith**. *Viaticum* is now understood as *the* last sacrament, and is administered *after* the **anointing of the sick**. Formerly, however, the anointing (once called **extreme unction**) was given last.

VIGIL (2) – A service held on the evening prior to a feast. The supreme vigil is that of **Easter**, held after sunset on Holy Saturday. Certain feasts have separate texts for a Mass celebrated on the vigil (e.g. Pentecost, June 24, August 15, December 25). Vigils of certain feasts were formerly days of **fast** and **abstinence**.

VIMPA (3) – A shoulder veil worn by special assistants at a **stational Mass**. In form it is similar to the humeral veil but usually much thinner and simpler. It is usually worn by the miter bearer and frequently by the crosier bearer as well. The ends of the *vimpa* are wrapped around the **miter** or **crosier** to prevent soiling.

VOCATION, SACRAMENTS OF (2) – A contemporary generic term applied to **matrimony, holy orders** and sometimes the **anointing of the sick**.

VOTIVE CANDLES (2) – Small candles set in a rack before altars, shrines or statues in some churches, and lighted by the faithful as a sign of their prayers.

VOTIVE MASS (2) – A Mass celebrated at the wish (in Latin, *votum*) of the presiding priest. The texts used are not those of the liturgical season or feast, but are taken from a selection of Masses honoring God (e.g. the Trinity, Christ, the Holy Spirit), or Mary, or the angels, or one of the saints. Sometimes, texts chosen from the "Masses for various needs and occasions" are also called *votive Masses*. (GIRM 329b, c)

WASHING OF FEET (2) – The (optional) rite imitating the Lord's action at the **Last Supper**. It may take place in the Roman Rite after the homily at the evening Mass of the Lord's Supper on **Holy Thursday**. In the Ambrosian Rite of Milan, if it takes place, the footwashing rite must be celebrated apart from Mass. It is sometimes called the **mandatum**. In the writings of **Ambrose**, a *washing of feet* of the newly-baptized is mentioned in connection with the baptismal liturgy.

WASHING OF HANDS (2) – The ritual cleansing that takes place during the **preparation of the gifts** after the bread and wine have been placed on the altar (and incensed). Originally a practical action, it is now a symbolic gesture reminiscent of baptismal purification. In the Tridentine Missal, the priest was directed to wash only his thumbs and the tips of his index fingers. These are the digits that touch the host and, according to the Tridentine Missal, had to touch each other after the consecration of the host until the **ablutions** after communion. The revised Missal directs the priest to wash his *hands* and not merely his fingertips. It is frequently called the **lavábo**. (GIRM 52, 106)

WATER (1) – The most plentiful object in God's material creation. It is used in various liturgies in different ways. Its most important use is for washing a person during the sacrament of **baptism**, a washing that symbolizes a plunge into the death of Christ. **Holy water** is frequently used as a reminder of baptism. During Mass, water (symbolically representing Christ's humanity) is used to dilute the wine (cf. **mixed chalice**). Water is also used by the priest to wash his hands after the preparation of gifts. Ideally, separate vessels of water are used for these two purposes during Mass. (GIRM 103, 106)

WATER, HOLY (1) – Water that has been specially blessed may be sprinkled on the assembly during the introductory rites of the Mass or other liturgies, a rite formerly called the **asperges.** *Holy water* is also usually stored in **stoups** at the entrances into a church so that individuals may bless themselves with it, reminding them of the waters of baptism. It is frequently used when a **blessing** of objects is celebrated.

WHITSUNDAY (3) – The common British term for **Pentecost**, used because those baptized at Easter wore their *white* garments again.

WINE (1) – Grape *wine* has been used at Mass following the Lord's actions at the Last Supper, since it is a traditional element used at Passover meals. By custom, some **water** is mixed with the wine when the cup is prepared before the eucharistic prayer. (See the entry on **mixed chalice** above.) (GIRM 284)

WORD OF GOD (2) – Another name for the **Bible**. Because of the first chapter of St. John's gospel, Jesus is also called the *Word of God.* (GIRM 8, 33, 34; LM 2)

WORSHIP (1) – The expression of our love, reverence, honor, and adoration of a good and gracious God through various communal and private activities. In general, in Christian tradition, the worshipping assembly prays *to* God (the Father), *through* Christ, empowered by (or *in the unity of*) the Spirit (cf. GIRM 32, the standard conclusion to the **collect**, and, e.g., Rom 1:8; 2 Cor 1:5, 3:4; Heb 13:15; 1 Pet 2:5). Expressions of public worship are not normally directed *to* Christ, and, in fact, the Council of Hippo in 393 forbade the direct addressing of Christ in public prayer. However, exceptions to this general rule exist in the Roman Mass where often the assembly as a whole prays to Christ (e.g. in the **Kyrie** or **Agnus Dei**), while the presiding priest normally prays to God (the Father) (e.g. the eucharistic prayer). However, there are exceptions to this general principle, as in the presidential prayer before the **sign of peace** (after the Lord's Prayer).

YEAR, LITURGICAL (1) – The annual cycle of events commemorated each year through various worship celebrations. The liturgical year of the Roman Rite begins with the First Sunday of Advent. It is divided into four major **seasons** centered around the celebrations of Christmas and Easter, and an additional general season called **Ordinary Time**. The liturgical year attempts to provide the same pattern of repetition needed for growth that the natural year provides.

ZIKKARON (3) – The Hebrew word for active remembering corresponding to the Greek word **anamnesis**.

ZONE (3) – The cloth waist belt made of the same material as the other major external **vestments**, worn by priests of the **Byzantine Rite** in place of the **cincture**.

ZUCCHETTO (2) – A skull cap. It is usually worn by those who have the right to wear a **miter**. In origin it was designed to protect the cloth of the miter from the natural oil of the hair. It is also worn by members of certain religious orders in certain countries. Also spelled *zuchetto* or called by the Latin word *pileolus*.

BIBLIOGRAPHY

With gratitude to E. D. Hirsch, Jr. for his thoughts about literacy, reference is first made to the major books related to *Cultural Literacy*.

Hirsch, E. D., Jr. *Cultural Literacy: What Every American Needs to Know.* Boston: Houghton Mifflin Co., 1987. (Clothbound)

Hirsch, E. D., Jr. *Cultural Literacy: What Every American Needs to Know.* New York: Random House (Vintage Books), 1988. (Paperback)

Hirsch, E. D., Jr., Kett, Joseph F., and Trefil, James. *The Dictionary of Cultural Literacy: What Every American Needs to Know.* Boston: Houghton Mifflin Co., 1988.

Zahler, Diane and Zahler, Kathy A. *Test Your Cultural Literacy.* New York: Arco, 1988.

An excellent bibliography of practical liturgical books was prepared by the Rev. William Marrevee for the Summer Institute in Pastoral Liturgy at Saint Paul University in Ottawa, Canada. That listing was printed in the Canadian periodical, the *National Bulletin on Liturgy* (vol. 20, May-June 1987, n. 109, pp. 134–150).

DICTIONARIES AND ENCYCLOPEDIAS

Attwater, Donald. *A Catholic Dictionary.* 2nd ed. New York: The Macmillan Co., 1954 (1949).

Broderick, Robert C. *The Catholic Encyclopedia.* Nashville: Thomas Nelson Inc., Publishers, 1976.

Davies, J. G. (ed.). *A Dictionary of Liturgy and Worship.* New York: The Macmillan Company, 1972.

Davies, J. G. (ed.). *The New Westminster Dictionary of Liturgy and Worship.* Philadelphia: The Westminster Press, 1986.

Komonchak, Joseph (ed.). *The New Dictionary of Theology.* Wilmington, Delaware: Michael Glazier, 1987.

Nevins, Albert J., M.M. (ed.). *The Maryknoll Catholic Dictionary.* New York: Grosset & Dunlap: Dimension Books, 1965.

New Catholic Encyclopedia. New York: McGraw Hill, 1967.

Podhradsky, Gerhard. *New Dictionary of the Liturgy.* Staten Island: Alba House, 1966.

MAJOR BOOKS AND BOOKLETS

Botte, Bernard, O.S.B. *From Silence to Participation: An Insider's View of Liturgical Renewal.* Washington: The Pastoral Press, 1988.

Bouyer, Louis. *Eucharist: Theology and Spirituality of the Eucharistic Prayer.* Notre Dame: University of Notre Dame Press, 1968.

Cabie, Robert. *The Eucharist* (Vol. II of *The Church At Prayer*) (new edition, 1986). Collegeville: The Liturgical Press, 1986.

Carroll, Thomas K. and Halton, Thomas. *Liturgical Practice in the Fathers*. Wilmington: Michael Glazier, 1988.

Casel, Odo, O.S.B. *The Mystery of Christian Worship*. Westminster: Newman Press, 1962.

Champlin, Joseph M. *The Proper Balance*. Notre Dame: Ave Maria Press, 1981.

Chupungco, Anscar J., O.S.B. *Cultural Adaptation in the Liturgy*. New York: Paulist Press, 1982.

Crichton, J.D. *Christian Celebration: The Mass / Sacraments / Prayer of the Church*. London: Geoffrey Chapman, 1971, 1973, 1976, 1979, 1981. (Available in three volumes, or in a one volume edition.)

Daniélou, Jean, S.J. *The Bible and the Liturgy*. Notre Dame: University of Notre Dame Press, 1956.

Diekmann, Godfrey, O.S.B. *Come, Let us Worship*. Baltimore: Helicon Press, 1964.

Directory for Masses with Children, Sacred Congregation for Divine Worship, November 1, 1973.

Dix, Gregory. *The Shape of the Liturgy*. Westminster: Dacre Press, 1945. (New edition with an updating appendix by: New York: Seabury, 1982.)

Documents on the Liturgy: 1963–1979—Conciliar, Papal, and Curial Texts. Collegeville: The Liturgical Press, 1982.

Douglas, Mary. *Natural Symbols: Explorations in Cosmology*. New York: Pantheon, 1970.

Eliade, Mircea. *The Sacred and the Profane: The Nature of Religion*. New York: Harper and Row, Publishers, 1959.

Ellard, Gerald, S.J. *The Mass in Transition*. Milwaukee: Bruce Publishing Co., 1956.

Emminghaus, Johannes H. *The Eucharist: Essence, Form, Celebration*. Collegeville: The Liturgical Press, 1978.

Environment and Art in Catholic Worship, Bishops' Committee on the Liturgy, National Conference of Catholic Bishops, 1978. Available from USCC Office of Publishing Services, Washington. A bilingual (Spanish) edition with revised photographs is available from Liturgy Training Publications: 1800 N. Hermitage Ave., Chicago, IL 60622 (312/486-7008).

Eucharistic Concelebration. Bishops' Committee on the Liturgy, Study Text 5.

Fitzgerald, George, C.S.P. *Handbook of the Mass*. New York: Paulist Press, 1982.

Fleming, Austin. *Preparing for Liturgy: A Theology and Spirituality*. Washington: The Pastoral Press, 1985.

Foley, Edward and McGann, Mary. *Music and the Eucharistic Prayer*. Washington: The Pastoral Press, 1988.

Fulfilled In Your Hearing: The Homily in the Sunday Assembly. Bishops' Committee on Priestly Life and Ministry, National Conference of Catholic Bishops, 1982.

Guzie, Tad W. *The Book of Sacramental Basics*. New York: Paulist Press, 1982.

Hovda, Robert W. *Strong, Loving and Wise: Presiding in Liturgy*. Collegeville: The Liturgical Press, 1976, 1980.

Huck, Gabe. *Liturgy with Style and Grace*. Chicago: Liturgy Training Publications, 1984.

Irwin, Kevin W. *Liturgy, Prayer, and Spirituality*. New York: Paulist Press, 1984.

Jones, Cheslyn, Wainwright, Geoffrey and Yarnold, Edward, S.J. (eds.). *The Study of Liturgy*. New York: Oxford University Press, 1978.

Jungmann, Joseph A., S.J. *The Mass of the Roman Rite*. 2 vols. New York: Benzinger, 1951. (a one volume edition was reprinted by Westminster: Christian Classics, 1974.)

Kavanagh, Aidan, O.S.B. *Elements of Rite: A Handbook of Liturgical Style*. New York: Pueblo Publishing Co., 1982.

Kavanagh, Aidan, O.S.B. *On Liturgical Theology*. New York: Pueblo Publishing Co., 1984.

Kay, Melissa (ed.). *It is Your Own Mystery: A Guide to the Communion Rite*. Washington: The Liturgical Press, 1977.

Keifer, Ralph A. *To Give Thanks and Praise*. Washington: National Association of Pastoral Musicians, 1980.

Kilmartin, Edward J., S.J. *Christian Liturgy: I. Theology*. Kansas City: Sheed and Ward, 1988.

Liturgical Music Today. Bishops' Committee on the Liturgy, National Conference of Catholic Bishops, 1982. USCC Office of Publishing Services. Publication No. 854.

Liturgy Planning. Minneapolis: Winston Press, 1983.

Mediator Dei, Encyclical letter of Pope Pius XII, November 20, 1947.

McKenna, John H., C.M. *Eucharist and Holy Spirit: The Eucharistic Epiclesis in 20th Century Theology.* Great Wakering: Mayhew-McCrimmon, Ltd., 1975.

McManus, Frederick R. (ed.). *Thirty Years of Liturgical Renewal: Statements of the Bishops' Committee on the Liturgy.* Washington: United States Catholic Conference, 1987.

Mitchell, Leonel L. *The Meaning of Ritual.* Wilton: Morehouse-Barlow, 1977 [1987].

Mitchell, Nathan, O.S.B. *Cult and Controversy: The Worship of the Eucharist Outside Mass.* New York: Pueblo Publishing Company, 1982.

Mueller, John Baptist, S.J. *Handbook of Ceremonies: For Priests and Seminarians.* St. Louis: B. Herder Book Co., 1958.

Music in Catholic Worship. Bishops' Committee on the Liturgy, National Conference of Catholic Bishops, Second Edition, 1983. USCC Office of Publishing Services. Publication No. 857.

The Mystery of Faith: A Study of the Structural Elements of the Order of Mass, The Federation of Diocesan Liturgical Commissions. Washington, 1980.

Nocent, Adrian, O.S.B. *The Liturgical Year.* Vols. 1–4. Collegeville: The Liturgical Press, 1977.

O'Connell, J. B. *The Celebration of Mass*. Milwaukee: The Bruce Publishing Co., 1964.

Otto, Rudolf. *The Idea of the Holy: An Inquiry into the Non-Rational in an Idea of the Divine and its Relation to the Rational*. London: Penguin, 1959.

Power, David N., O.M.I. *Unsearchable Riches: The Symbolic Nature of the Liturgy*. New York: Pueblo Publishing Company, 1984.

A Reader: The Environment for Worship. Bishops' Committee on the Liturgy, National Conference of Catholic Bishops, 1980.

Schmemann, Alexander. *The Eucharist: Sacrament of the Kingdom*. Crestwood: St. Vladimir's Seminary Press, 1988.

Schmemann, Alexander. *Introduction to Liturgical Theology*. 3rd ed. Crestwood: St. Vladimir's Seminary Press, 1986.

Searle, Mark. *Liturgy Made Simple*. Collegeville: The Liturgical Press, 1981.

Smolarski, Dennis C., S.J. *Eucharistia: A Study of the Eucharistic Prayer*. New York: Paulist Press, 1982.

Smolarski, Dennis C., S.J. *How not To Say Mass*. New York: Paulist Press, 1986.

Stevenson, Kenneth. *Jerusalem Revisited: The Liturgical Meaning of Holy Week*. Washington: The Pastoral Press, 1988.

Talley, Thomas J. *The Origins of the Liturgical Year*. New York: Pueblo Publishing Company, 1986.

Bibliography

This Holy and Living Sacrifice: Directory for the Celebration and Reception of Communion under Both Kinds. National Conference of Catholic Bishops, Nov 1, 1984.

Turner, Victor W. *The Ritual Process: Structure and Anti-Structure.* London: Routledge and Kegan Paul, 1969.

Vagaggini, Cyprian, O.S.B. *Theological Dimensions of the Liturgy: A General Treatise on the Theology of the Liturgy.* Collegeville: The Liturgical Press, 1976.

Walsh, Eugene A., S.S. *From Rubrics to Ritual: Celebrating the Difference!* Daytona Beach: Pastoral Arts Associates of North America, 1988.

Walsh, Eugene A., S.S. *Giving Life: The Ministry of the Parish Sunday Assembly.* Daytona Beach, FL: Pastoral Arts Associates of North America, 1985.

Walsh, Eugene A., S.S. *The Order of Mass: Guidelines.* Daytona Beach, FL: Pastoral Arts Associates of North America, 1979, 1981, 1986.

Walsh, Eugene A., S.S. *Practical Suggestions for Celebrating Sunday Mass.* Daytona Beach, FL: Pastoral Arts Associates of North America, 1978, 1981, 1986.

Wegman, Herman. *Christian Worship in East and West: A Study Guide to Liturgical History.* New York: Pueblo Publishing Company, 1985.

Wilkinson, John. *Egeria's Travels.* 2nd ed. Jerusalem/Warminster: Ariel, 1981.

Willimon, William H. *Word, Water, Wine and Bread: How Worship Has Changed over the Years.* Valley Forge: Judson Press, 1980.

The official introductions to the liturgical books can also be obtained in the latest revised editions from various sources.

General Instruction of the Liturgy of the Hours. Washington: USCC, 1983. Publication No. 898 (Liturgy Documentary Series 5).

General Instruction of the Roman Missal [from second *editio typica* of the Roman Missal (1975)] Washington: USCC, 1982. Publication No. 852 (Liturgy Documentary Series 2).

General Norms for the Liturgical Year and the Calendar, found in *Norms Governing Liturgical Calendars.* Washington: USCC, 1984. Publication No. 928 (Liturgy Documentary Series 6).

Lectionary for Mass: Introduction [from second *editio typica* of the Lectionary for Mass (1981)] Washington: USCC, 1981. Publication No. 839 (Liturgy Documentary Series 1).

PERIODICALS—YEARLY BOOKLETS

Liturgy 90. Chicago: Liturgy Training Publications.

National Bulletin on the Liturgy. Canadian Conference of Catholic Bishops, 90 Parent Ave., Ottawa, Ontario, K1N 7B1 Canada.

Newsletter, Bishops' Committee on the Liturgy. USCC, 1312 Massachusetts Ave., N.W., Washington, DC 20005.

Sourcebook for Sundays and Seasons. Chicago: Liturgy Training Publications.

Worship. Published at St. John's Abbey, Collegeville, Minnesota 56321.

BV
173
.S66
1990